Classroom to Workplace

Classroom to Workplace

Land Your First Marketing Communications Job

Lynn Appelbaum

┃┃╻BEP

(BUSINESS EXPERT PRESS Q)

Leader in applied, concise business books

First published in 2024 by
Business Expert Press, LLC
222 East 46th Street, New York, NY 10017
www.businessexpertpress.com

ISBN-13: 978-1-63742-726-2 (paperback)
ISBN-13: 978-1-63742-727-9 (e-book)

Business Expert Press Business Career Development Collection

First edition: 2024

10 9 8 7 6 5 4 3 2 1

For Joe, Shosha and Elana, and my amazing students

Description

Classroom to Workplace: Land Your First Marketing Communications Job **is the perfect career-building handbook for those entering the marketing communications professions.** It provides practical guidance and easy-to-use motivational steps to help advertising, public relations, and digital marketing students and grads chart their own path to overcome insecurities and job-hunting roadblocks, putting their best foot forward starting now.

Featuring valuable insights from diverse communications majors who have landed competitive jobs, the book offers proven tips to help aspiring professionals manage nerves and self-doubt, choose career directions, get the most from internships, build a professional network, craft application materials, interview confidently, and start strong in a new job. Hiring and human resource professionals share essential best practices for success.

Contents

Testimonials

"**Classroom to Workplace** *is an indispensable 'yes you can' guide for college students embarking on their professional journeys. Professor Appelbaum's expertise as a tenured teacher and communications professional shines on every page, making this book a compassionate companion for jittery students hoping for a seamless transition from the classroom to their first professional role. With its practical and empathetic advice, engaging stories from students who have been there, and wealth of contemporary tips and resources, this book is a fountain of encouragement and a must read for serious students ready to take charge of their careers.*"—**Grace Leong, Chief Executive Officer, HUNTER**

"*Lynn Appelbaum is the professor we all dream of: honest and practical, tough and fair, generous and inclusive. Her wisdom is rooted in a career of **doing**, equaled only by an epic second act in the classroom. As an educator, Appelbaum catalyzed the careers of thousands of college students—many the first in their family to graduate—and at least one nonprofit dedicated to this mission. Now, **miraculously**, she's captured all this wisdom in a deeply engaging book that's as honest, practical, and inclusive as its author. Starting your career can be hard, lonely, and sometimes bewildering. Appelbaum doesn't sugarcoat this: she tells it as it is, but always with a clear call to action—and always by sharing her platform with the voices of former students thriving in careers of their own. Above all else,* **Classroom to Workplace** *left me with a palpable sense of **momentum**. Read this book and set yourself in motion.*"—**Kalani Leifer, Founder & CEO, COOP Careers**

"*Lynn Appelbaum is a superstar in academia and everything you want in a professor. She has a great track record of supporting and mentoring students as a PRSSA Faculty Adviser and been instrumental in the launch of hundreds of careers in communications.* **Classroom to Workplace** *is a must read for anyone navigating the transition from student to professional, backed by decades of experience and first-hand knowledge.*"—**Jeneen Garcia, Senior Vice President of Programs, Public Relations Society of America**

"*Lynn Appelbaum's deep personal and professional empathy for and experience with those seeking their first job in marketing communications builds a connection with the reader from page one. Her honest reflection on her own job search and the inclusion of enlightening perspectives from her former students about how they found their place in the industry make the book as much a confidence builder as it is a crystal-clear roadmap for securing that first job. 'Read* **Classroom to Workplace**' *is now my first piece of advice for all recent graduates. Like Lynn, it's the real deal.*"—**Kathleen Donohue Rennie, PhD, APR, Fellow PRSA, Chair, Integrated Marketing and Communications, New York University, School of Professional Studies**

"*Lynn Appelbaum has given students moving from campus to workplace the handbook they need to navigate an increasingly complex business landscape. I can't think of a better guide for students making the life-altering transition to entry-level professional than* **Classroom to Workplace: Land Your First Marketing Communications Job**. *Lynn's years of experience as a trusted counselor to thousands of students, most of whom were not blessed with power at birth, and a leading voice for increasing diversity and inclusion in the industry are the foundation for her uniquely wise and thorough approach to not only landing that first job, but building the networks and knowledge critical to sustaining a career. Advice and perspectives from former students of diverse backgrounds, as well as HR professionals and others address concerns about life in the working world in ways that are candid, relatable, and invaluable.*"—**Judith Harrison, Chief Diversity, Equity and Inclusion Officer, Weber Shandwick**

"*Recent graduates owe Lynn Appelbaum a debt of gratitude. This book takes the mystery out of the transition between college and the workplace by creating an easy-to-understand process that I am certain will help many get their careers started. Breaking down the advice into specific suggestions and tactics is a unique and useful approach new job seekers will appreciate tremendously.*"—**Belle Frank, Chief Strategy Officer Emeritus, VML Health Practice, Author of *The Advertising On-Ramp: Getting Your First Job in Advertising***

Acknowledgments

I owe my deepest gratitude to many people who played a role in this book's creation and completion. They gave me support, encouragement, and ideas to make this a better book than I alone could have created.

Thanks to Scott Isenberg and the superb team at BEP for making this book a reality. Your affirming response was a dream come true and inspired me to go beyond my original vision for this book. I am indebted to you for all your support.

To Michelle Rapkin and Susan Badger: This book would not have seen the light of day without your help. Michelle, my lifelong friend, an outstanding publishing professional, and an early supporter of this project, introduced me to Susan, who used her extraordinary guidance and network to help me find a publisher in BEP. Your essential roles are a testament to the power of networking, and, even more, to a deep and enduring friendship.

To Gail Belmuth and Donna Renella, dear friends whom I respect so much as professionals. You gave me important and substantive feedback and inspired me to make this a better book. Throughout you listened and cheered me on, just like you do in the rest of my life.

Deepest thanks to Belle Frank, Chief Strategy Officer Emeritus, VML whom I hold in the highest regard and who knows what it takes to be successful in this industry. I am so grateful for your expert and honest critique.

Thank you, Jeneen Garcia, Judith Harrison, Grace Leong, and Kathleen Donohue Rennie for being extraordinary industry colleagues throughout my career as an educator, and for your generous support of this book.

To Jody Karg for sharing your essential, candid feedback from a young professional's perspective. Your contributions were invaluable and are reflected throughout these pages.

To my former students who contributed inspiring wisdom through-out the book. I felt the luckiest to be your teacher years ago, but I am even luckier to see who you are today, personally and professionally. You are savvier than I was early in my career, and it is inspiring to watch your trajectory. Thank you: Susan Akinyi-Tindi, Mushfiqa Andalib, Ari Berkowitz, Heather Lynn Burnside, Domonique Chaplin, Esraa Elzin, Genesis Flores, Luis Herrera, Kezia Kent, Jerry Louis, Erika Sanchez, Isabella Santana, Anne Tan-Detchkov, and Ibrahim Tatlicioglu, for helping me to "show" beyond "tell" through your own powerful experiences in transitioning to the workplace.

To the superb human resource and DEI professionals and advisers who contributed so much to this book. Thank you: Rhea Faniel, Tasha Gilroy, Allyns Melendez, Melanie Rakita, and Andrea Weinzimer. You contributed essential perspectives as professionals who understand what it takes to be successful in a competitive workplace. My gratitude to Tracey Wood Mendelsohn and Ashley Orlando for your valuable insights.

To my husband Joe Spivack: Long before this book was even a thought, you were my constant support and champion who helped me to push through the hard times to succeed even when I doubted myself. Your substantive contributions and wisdom throughout have made this book far better than I, alone, could have delivered. Your always loving, constructive, and incisive feedback gave me confidence and inspired me to deliver the best work I could. This book and my life are better because of you.

Beyond this book, I celebrate those who played essential roles in helping me achieve my dreams and whose wisdom is reflected herein. I am indebted to my parents, Sidney and Sylvia Appelbaum (*in memoriam*), my constant role models and champions, and to others who impacted my career and life in powerful ways: Stuart Dim (*in memoriam*), Eileen Gilmartin (*in memoriam*), Helen Horowitz, and Ziva Kwitney.

The City College of New York (CCNY) was my professional home for 27 years. I am grateful to all those who share their dedication to our students, especially my communications colleagues: Gerardo Blumenkrantz, Javier Garcia, Ed Keller, Lynne Scott Jackson, and Nancy Tag; and to Moe Liu-D'Albero, Leslie Galman, and Elena Sturman for your friendship and unflagging support. Dot Giannone (*in memoriam*), former EVP at VMLY&R, opened a powerful pipeline for many talented and diverse students to internships and jobs. You played a transformative role in the lives of so many of my students, and in mine. To Helen Shelton, Global Chief Diversity and Inclusion Officer at Finn Partners, thank you for your vision and support of young talent.

To Rochelle Ford, PhD and Frank Walton, PhD: Thank you for being extraordinary colleagues and partners in our research studies about the experience of multicultural professionals in the workplace. These findings inform some key insights in this book.

My PRSA-NY colleagues were instrumental in helping me to succeed once I started my teaching career, and have enriched my life in powerful ways. Deepest thanks to Carol Davis-Grossman, Roberta Elins, Sandra Fathi, Henry Feintuch, Lea-Ann Germinder, Leslie Gottlieb, and especially Art Stevens for serving as stellar professional role models and for always lending a helping hand to my students and me. You inspired me to be a better professional, and you gave so much to my students.

Kalani Leifer, founder of COOP Careers, is an inspiration. Your cold-call in 2014 to pitch CCNY's Ad/PR program as the incubator for COOP was a godsend to my students. I had the good sense to say, "yes!" Today, COOP has paved the way for thousands of young professionals to transition to digital marketing and other careers. Some of this book's core content was developed for my presentations to COOP Fellows. Thanks to Jennifer Matos for inviting me to remain a part of this dynamic program.

Thank you, Jasmine Martin and Leanna Pham, former students, now awesome professionals for helping to spread the word.

To my family and friends who sustain me, I'm beyond grateful to have you in my life. Thank you for being my champions through the kvetch and kvell.

To my daughters, Shosha and Elana Spivack: It was always my joy and pride to take you to City College on "Take Your Daughter to Work Day." Having you meet my students was the perfect blending of the families that I love. I am beyond proud of you: amazing women with heart, intelligence, and grace. I would not be the person or teacher I am without you.

My heartfelt thanks to all—Lynn Appelbaum

Introduction

This book is inspired by and based on what I have learned from my own journey as a public relations (PR) practitioner and professor.

Throughout my 27 years on the Advertising/PR faculty at The City College of New York (CCNY), I had the privilege of teaching and mentoring hundreds of students during their journey from the classroom to the professional workplace.

Each student inspired me with their intelligence, heart, and drive, using their CCNY education as a springboard to a profession, most often in marketing communications. They shared their dreams and their challenges, some formidable. I worked with a variety of students, some who could dedicate themselves full-time to school, others who had to work part-time and attend school while caring for family, and other older students who returned to college to relaunch their careers. Each had their own hurdles, but what they all had in common was having to figure out how to use their marketing communications education as a springboard to the professional world. It was exciting and scary. How could they gain confidence, make the transition from student to professional, and be successful? What lay ahead felt daunting.

Many students, as the first in their family to earn a college degree, felt a great burden to succeed in the professional arena, having no family or mentors to point the way. They placed their trust in me, allowing themselves to be vulnerable and candid about their insecurities and self-doubts, so we could work together to showcase their best selves and to move forward with greater self-confidence and courage. Their success was always reason to celebrate.

This book offers more guidance than I, alone, could offer. Throughout, you'll hear the voices of former students of diverse backgrounds who were extraordinary when I taught them, and are even more so now as professionals who successfully transitioned from student to workplace. Hearing how they navigated their journey and overcame challenges is inspiring. I hope they can be role models for you.

You'll also hear from outstanding human resource (HR) professionals, recruiters, and advisers who share their wisdom and insights that come with a deep understanding of workplace demands and stem from years of nurturing young professionals to succeed.

Besides learning from my students, I gained wisdom from my earlier experience, including 14 years as a PR professional prior to becoming a professor. As a young woman coming of age in the 1970s, professional role models were hard to find. I and most of my generation were paving new ground in the job market dominated mostly by men. We had to figure things out for ourselves, frequently the hard way, often not pleasant. When I became a professor, I made a commitment to myself to become the mentor to my students that I never had when I was starting out. I knew what it felt like to feel insecure about my abilities, to be clueless about what I was best suited to do, and how to build a professional life.

I did not start out wanting to be a public relations professional or a college professor. I dreamed of becoming the conductor of the New York Philharmonic (not too grandiose)! But, like many, I learned that where you start is not always where you end up. There are so many factors that impact our direction, cause us to rethink our choices, and shape the course of our careers. Perhaps you can relate this to your own experience.

As a PR professional who transitioned to teaching, I feel strongly that I ended up in an ideal place where I could share my passion for media with students I adored and where I could be of value in ways I had never dreamed of. I even got to fulfill my earliest dream of conducting, albeit not at the New York Philharmonic, when one of my film colleagues, Andrzej Krakowski, observed my class and wrote that he felt like he was watching a masterful conductor. So, for me, it all came full circle, although in ways I never could have predicted.

This book is for those students and professionals who might benefit from my years mentoring and inspiring young talent. It is my hope that some of the guidance within these pages will ease your path by providing honest insights and helpful advice on your journey to launch and build a rewarding career. Here we go!

Lynn Appelbaum

CHAPTER 1

Owning Your Story, Celebrating Your Brand

A journey of a thousand miles begins with a single step.

—Lao Tsu

Where are you on your professional journey? Most of the students I worked with were diverse college juniors or seniors—full-time students taking classes in The City College of New York (CCNY) Advertising/PR major, working part-time in retail or food service to support themselves and maybe their families. They knew they wanted to get a job in marketing communications, but they saw no clear path forward.

Others, whom I mentored from the COOP Careers program, were recent college grads, or those with degrees in other majors or careers, who were transitioning to marketing communications. They were just beginning to attain the prerequisite skills through the intensive workshops and professional mentoring that COOP offers.

Many students knew they needed to get an internship or an entry-level job to start building their professional credentials, but were hesitant to apply because they didn't feel competitive. Some were afraid to choose any direction for fear of missing out on what they didn't apply for. Some were terrified of rejection. Others didn't know how they could possibly fit in another responsibility to an already overflowing schedule juggling school, work, family obligations, and commuting. If they were the first generation in their family to go to college and/or were multicultural, many felt burdened by additional challenges, having had no professional role models. They felt stuck, lost, scared or a combination of all three.

Working with students or transitioning professionals, such as yourself, I begin with the basics to identify key personal attributes that make you a desirable and competitive professional. We focus on how to stop thinking about yourself as an insecure student and to start acknowledging your qualities that support your professionalism. This can open many doors.

Your success starts with how YOU see yourself and what you have to offer. If you have the determination to move forward despite your fears and self-doubt, here's a high five! Keep reading.

Perspectives: Rhea Faniel, Senior Associate Director, Diversity Recruitment and Employer Relations, The City College of New York

Many students let their own insecurities and fears stop them from applying for internships or jobs, because they do not believe they have skills that employers want, when they actually do. Students sometimes do not give themselves enough credit for the value of their experience, including in retail or as a server, where delivering customer service is essential. This is transferable to so many professions. It's a matter of valuing your own experience and reframing it for the workplace so you can showcase your value to an employer.

The most important thing students need to consider when thinking about a career is not to limit themselves. Marketing communications majors have lots of job options because they have strong oral and written communication skills and know how to connect with different audiences. You may start out wanting to be an ad copywriter, but there are many other ways to use creative skills in industries such as banking, publishing, or media. Communication is transferable to related careers such as client/customer relations, too. So, explore all your options!

Use sites such as mediabistro.com, joblist.com, and bookjobs.com, beyond LinkedIn and Indeed.com to research jobs. Take advantage of campus outreach programs such as Vox Media's Breaking Media, NeilsenIQ University, or NBCUniversal's Academy offerings that especially target diverse college students for specialized skills building.

If you are not sure your campus offers these programs, ask your campus career office.

What's Your Professional Brand?

For starters, begin thinking of yourself as your personal client. Your objective: to launch your career with a competitive internship or entry-level job. Before you begin actively applying for jobs, you want to identify your "professional brand." This is *not the totality* of who you are, but rather the parts of you that you want to showcase to prospective employers. This includes your unique and desirable attributes that celebrate your value and distinguish you as a potential employee.

While your professional brand assets will change as you grow professionally, these are not "aspirational." Think about attributes and skills that you are confident you now possess and for which you can show evidence. To talk confidently to employers about what you offer, you must first "own" your skills and attributes yourself.

Creating Your Own SWOT Analysis for Your Professional Brand—Are You Ready?

Any good marketing plan has a strong strategic foundation that is built on understanding what makes a brand unique and valuable to your target audience. In this case, it's what makes *you* valuable to *prospective employers*. See Figure 1.1.

Typically, marketing strategic planning includes a **SWOT analysis:**

Strengths: Your essential attributes that speak to your professionalism;

Weaknesses: Areas that you acknowledge need improvement;

Opportunities: Elements of the business environment that can work to your advantage;

Threats: Elements of the business environment that can impede your success.

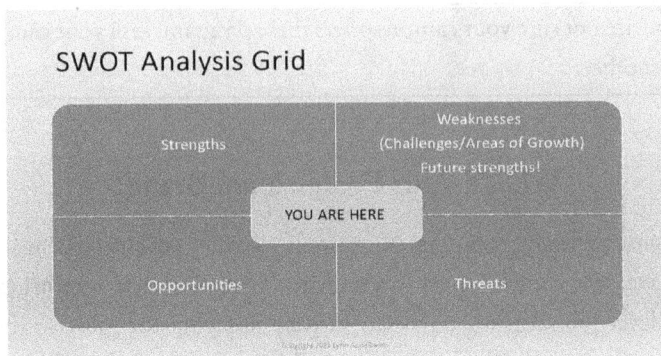

Figure 1.1 SWOT analysis grid

Strengths

Your strengths include *personal* **and/or** *professional attributes* that prospective employers will find desirable. It's important to identify strengths that help you stand out in your own right. Many students enter the workplace describing their strengths as being smart, motivated, and eager to learn. That's a start, but it's not enough. You want to identify your *specific* attributes that capture what you bring to a job. Here's your chance to build *your* brand.

Think about your personal attributes as soft skills that showcase your maturity and work ethic, such as being reliable, hardworking, professional, and a good communicator.

Remember, you don't need to be strong in *every* area. An honest reflection about your strengths and weaknesses is important to help you determine what types of jobs you might best be suited for, and, also, what kinds of jobs to avoid. It's also the foundation for how you present yourself to prospective employers.

Personal attributes might include:

Smart	Hardworking	Professional	Detail-oriented
Proactive	Curious	Results-driven	Tenacious
Multitasker	Team player	Self-directed	Takes initiative
Flexible	Overcomes obstacles	Passionate	Positive

Professional strengths are workplace skills that relate to the job you are applying for and that showcase your ability to be successful in the workplace.

These might include:

- **Prior work experience**—customer service, retail, caregiver: work that shows responsibility and/or a record of success.
- **Related experience**—internships and/or freelance experience.
- **Software skills**—Microsoft Office, Excel, Google AdWords, Cision, Canva, Adobe InDesign/Photoshop, data analytics, and database management.
- **Strong bilingual skills** that allow you to speak and write professionally in more than one language.
- **Strategic planning experience**—corporate communications, advertising management or planning, and digital marketing.
- **Project management experience**—can see a project successfully through to completion on deadline while multitasking numerous facets.
- **Problem-solving** that helps an employer meet or exceed business goals.
- **Research**—ability to find substantive information and glean insights.
- **Writing experience**—business communications—or a strong social-media driver.
- **Club leadership/teamwork**—can include college or community experience.

Owning Your Strengths

Take a few moments to reflect. Make a written list of your top personal and professional strengths that you are confident you possess.

Do *not* inflate your true value by claiming that you have an attribute that you don't actually have. This is your time to take stock of what you really bring, so be honest with yourself.

In my experience, some students have a hard time getting started identifying and celebrating their strengths due to insecurity. If you are feeling this, that's okay. Get quiet and start with what you really know about yourself. Other traits will come to you.

If you can't think of any specific strengths, talk to a professor, counselor, friend, or mentor who knows you. Ask them to identify what they see as your strengths and the traits that help you stand out. Then spend some time getting comfortable with these traits so that you are secure in knowing that you really bring these qualities to the workplace.

The strengths that you identify now as part of your brand can give you a powerful inspiration to get started. Keep in mind that celebrating these qualities will also fuel you in the longer term. These will change and grow throughout your career.

Self-Reflection: Workshop Your Strengths

The top four personal and professional strengths that I want to celebrate and reflect as part of my professional brand are:

Personal:

Professional:

Now, visualize each of these traits as a part of you. Imagine this trait inside you as a tangible part of your body, as you would, say, your heart. This way, when you talk about yourself to prospective employers, you can more easily own this trait with confidence and can support it with examples from your life.

Weaknesses

Whether we like to think about this or not, we all have weaknesses—areas that would benefit from improvement. While it may not be easy, acknowledging them will help you address them before you are actively interviewing and make it easier to answer questions later. Naming your challenges that may impede your success helps identify areas of targeted growth and prepares you to be even more competitive.

Possible Weaknesses That May Hold You Back

- I feel nervous about what I don't know, so I avoid applying for opportunities.
- I feel insecure about being competitive for an internship or job and think that others are so much more qualified, so I avoid opportunities.
- I tend to be shy and/or introverted.
- I lack experience in marketing communications/digital media.
- I have no other work experience or no other relevant work experience.
- I lack foundational skills that I know most jobs require, such as Excel proficiency.
- I'm not strong in oral and/or written communication.
- I don't have experience working in teams.
- I have a hard time following direction.
- I am careless with my work, or am often late with assignments or with other life commitments.

Perspectives: Susan Akinyi-Tindi, Account Director, Dieste Health

Even though it was hard to hear critical comments about my early resume drafts, being pushed prepared me for tough feedback in the workplace. My professors used constructive criticism to build me up, not tear me down, even if I'm my own biggest critic. Resilience is a big part of success for anyone, but especially for me as a woman of color. As an international student from Kenya, I put extra pressure on myself to do well. I wanted to build a career in the United States. A key thing I did as a student was to learn more from professors in my major about opportunities and competitive demands in my field that could affect getting a job in marketing communications. Success takes persistence, hard work, and belief in yourself.

My professors and capstone client project taught me that if I could push through the hard work in college, I could overcome obstacles in the workplace. Even if everyone on the team has a specific job, you need to be nimble and flexible. You can't always count on others. Sometimes you just have to rely on yourself.

What If I Feel Shy or Introverted?

Many students wonder if marketing communications is a good career fit for them, especially if they are shy or introverted. While that depends on the individual, it's helpful to know that marketing communications jobs, especially in agencies, generally attract professionals who thrive in dynamic, fast-paced environments, are social and adept at teamwork, and can work with varied and sometimes demanding clients. Alternatively, not-for-profit organizations or smaller organizations may be a better fit for those who might feel more comfortable in a less dynamic environment.

If you experience yourself as shy, use your passion for marketing communications to fuel your social growth starting now. Feeling shy is not a reason to change majors. Acknowledging this now presents an opportunity to build your confidence by participating more in class, joining clubs, and getting involved in outside organizations where you can practice being more engaged in social settings. Your aim is to become more at ease around others, get comfortable sharing your ideas, advocate for yourself, and develop your social skills. You are *not* trying to become someone you are not but rather are working at being a stronger and more comfortable communicator.

You can practice being more social by role playing your more extroverted side in the mirror, or by practicing with a friend—make eye contact, shake hands, and introduce yourself with conviction. It's never too early to go for your Oscar®! Role playing is a great way to practice being your more "social self."

Addressing Your Weaknesses (Challenges)

Just as it's important to celebrate your strengths, it's also important to assess the areas where you might need improvement and to acknowledge what is *within your control* that is holding you back.

Start with two challenges that you face. It could be a hurdle, like feeling insecure. Or you can think about some skill-based areas that you need to improve on, such as Excel skills. Remember, understanding your weaknesses can also help you steer clear of jobs that do not play to your best professional self. For example, if you are not detail-oriented, you'll probably want to steer away from jobs such as project management or data analytics, which require scrupulous attention to detail and excellent multitasking.

Once you identify one or two weaknesses, consider how you can begin to address your challenges. Remember, you are not trying to be perfect, but you do want to take action to improve, especially if you know that this is an important skill to land a job in marketing communications. It can be any committed action to help you address the challenge at hand, such as taking a course to help build proficiency in an area where you have a deficit or being proactive about joining a student club leadership team.

The key is not only acknowledging important challenges but also committing to an action that will help you feel stronger about the weakness.

Self-Reflection: Workshop Your Weaknesses

Two weaknesses that may be impacting my moving forward are:

These are the steps I will take to begin to address them:

Celebrate Being a Lifelong Learner

While many students count the days until they are no longer in school working under assignment deadlines, the truth is that in today's fast-changing technological workplace, competitive marketing professionals need to be lifelong learners. There is always more to learn to help you and your employer stay abreast of industry trends and changes. While you can expect to master the core aspects of your job with time, truly dynamic professionals are curious and are always learning. Plus, the ability to keep learning and growing is itself a crucial job skill, and, in fact, a crucial life skill too!

That means *getting comfortable with being uncomfortable* since a degree of discomfort often goes hand-in-hand with learning.

Perspectives: Kezia Kent, Senior, The City College of New York, Double Major: Economics, Advertising/PR; Intern, The TASC Group

I'm often afraid to try new things, but I don't let that stop me. When something doesn't work out, I try to learn from it and move on. Despite feeling insecure, I applied to a competitive fellowship even though I thought others had more impressive resumes. But I got it! I was passionate about the issue and could show how my personal experience added value.

I discovered the Ad/PR program by accident when I took Intro to Media. I was nervous about the major because I did not feel I was creative enough. I learned that creativity comes in many forms. I'm a good writer who can conceptualize ideas and explain them clearly to others, which has helped me succeed in many ways.

Developing self-discipline is one of the most important ways I've grown. I make a plan to accomplish everything on my list. Sometimes I still need to give myself a break, catch my breath, and get centered, especially when I'm facing rejection. If all else fails, I call my parents or a friend for a pick-me-up, or get a Starbucks and watch a movie until I'm ready to dig in again.

Staying aware of professional opportunities is another way I develop myself. Checking my college e-mail regularly helps me plug into opportunities such as internships, workshops, and networking events. I also get involved by joining community organizations whose missions I care about, such as the environment and social justice. This also helps me highlight my value beyond just my skills.

Beginner's Heart

Even now, when I embark on a new project and don't have a sense of mastery, I get nervous. You may feel this way when you start an internship, a new job, or even an unfamiliar project. There is a certain level of excitement about starting a new job when everything is before you, but there is also the fear of the unknown and whether you will be successful or not.

One antidote for this kind of discomfort is to embrace your *beginner's heart*.

Give yourself permission to be excited even if you may be afraid of failure. Some people think of this fear as the *imposter syndrome*, secretly fearful that they are not truly qualified to do a good job, when in fact, they have what it takes to succeed, but they let their fear take control.

Beginner's heart means:

It's okay to be afraid of the unknown.
It's okay to not feel confident.
It's okay to make some mistakes starting out.
It's okay to not have all the answers.

Try not to judge yourself too harshly. Trust that you will feel more comfortable and competent with time and practice.

Try to remember that just because you feel this way now, *it doesn't mean your present discomfort is permanent, or is a reflection of your future capabilities.*

Opportunities

Opportunities are circumstances or prospects that may benefit you in your immediate environment (your educational institution, your workplace, the marketing industry, and the larger world), to enhance your professional development.

That means paying attention to opportunities that you may not have considered, but which might enhance your experience, assist you with mentorship, job leads, or support to develop your professional self. These might include taking minor or elective classes in an area that expands on your communications studies. For example, you might consider taking some business classes to give you insights into business operations, marketing, or how the economic environment affects businesses. After all, communications play an essential role in helping businesses to meet their objectives. Business classes underscore that you are interested in, and understand, the bigger picture. Likewise, if you are creatively inclined, you might go deeper into digital and graphic design or video production to build on your skills as a content creator, or into another area that highlights your passion and depth of knowledge in a particular industry or area that you find exciting.

Perspectives: Ibrahim Tatlicioglu, Media Planning Supervisor, EssenceMediacom

College is a low-stakes playground. Take advantage of every resource and opportunity your college offers, especially networking events with professionals in the field. Talking to professionals you don't know can be nerve-wracking at first, but you have to learn to do it. You'll be doing it constantly in the workplace.

As a student, one of the most important ways I wish I had done better was understanding the nuances between media department jobs, what differentiates their roles, and how they fit together. While my classes covered the basics, I didn't really grasp the differences between media planning, media investment, and activation teams, for example. Each requires different skill sets and an understanding of how they mesh. When I first started out, that would have helped me figure out what I was good at, what I needed to do better, and what direction I should take.

I also wish I had realized sooner that creativity is essential for all communications roles, not just for agency "creatives" who write ads. That can really open up your thinking for lots of different communication options. For me, being a media planner means being curious, immersing myself in the industry, understanding and analyzing the data, and following marketplace trends to help my team deliver great work for clients.

Many students don't take advantage of "low hanging fruit," activities within easy reach, such as engaging with on-campus services, student clubs, professional organizations, professor networking, or even online groups to help fuel their growth. Take time to think about opportunities that may benefit you. Try to do some research outside of your day-to-day routine, and "cast a wider net" by considering some opportunities where the connection to your most direct career path may be a little less obvious.

Taking advantage of opportunities means it's up to you to be proactive and seek them out. Here are some possibilities you may not have thought of:

- Join a professional student club, such as the Public Relations Student Society of America (PRSSA), or American Advertising Federation (AAF), or others related to your interest or passion.
- Connect with local chapters of the Black Public Relations Society or the Hispanic Public Relations Association and other mentoring and professional development programs for multicultural students. (See Appendix.)

- Apply to the Multicultural Advertising Internship Program (MAIP), Emma Bowen Foundation, LAGRANT Foundation, T Howard Foundation, or IRTS Foundation for scholarship and/or internships. (See Appendix for more ideas.)
- Make an appointment to meet with your on-campus career counselors to research internships or jobs.
- Be attuned to announcements your professors make in class that could benefit you.
- Find a mentor: Proactively seek out professors or other professional contacts for their ideas and feedback on what you can do to begin to get experience and build a resume.
- If there is a professor who knows your work, this might be a good opportunity to ask them for their feedback on how you can strengthen your skills, share their assessment of your strengths, and help you to clarify a good direction for your first internship.
- The industry is growing quickly and needs skilled, diverse professionals. Look for organizations where your life experience and background could help the client.
- Start-ups are often looking for energetic, go-getter pros to help with marketing efforts.
- Take advantage of LinkedIn and other professional online networking groups.
- Consider taking workshops in a specific area through professional development organizations such as General Assembly, or get your certification in Google Analytics or other areas of professional expertise.
- Stay abreast of industry trends by reading at least one or more related trade publications such as *eMarketer, TechCrunch, The Verge, Digiday, AdWeek, Ad Age, SmartBrief, PR Week, PRovoke Media,* or others.

Self-Reflection: Workshop Your Opportunities

Conduct your own research. Look into some of the opportunities mentioned previously. What opportunities can you tap into that you may not have considered?

Make a list of opportunities that you can investigate to expand your professional reach. What tangible steps will you take to be more proactive?

Threats

Threats are circumstances in the industry and marketplace that are beyond your control, but which could impact your success. While you can't control threats, you will be better off being aware of the wider world outside of your own experience. These might include:

- Being aware that the competition is formidable, and also considering what you can do to help yourself stand out.
- Keeping abreast of hiring trends in the marketplace. Where are the jobs and the sectors where you are more likely to find openings?
- Being aware of your own responsibilities that may adversely impact your ability to dedicate time and energy to your job

hunt. How can you create time and space to effectively conduct your job search?

Self-Reflection: Workshop Your Threats

List some of the factors in the communications industry, the marketplace, or in your personal life, that are beyond your control, but that could impact your success. Talk to a professor, career adviser, or other mentor to better understand the hiring landscape and how this could impact your career direction. You can't change external factors, but it's better to be aware of challenges that may impact your search.

What steps can you take to mitigate external factors or others that could work against you?

Chapter Wrap Up

Congratulations! You just took some important steps on your journey to start thinking of yourself as a professional.

- You identified your core skills and qualities that will make you a competitive professional, and you have begun to "own" these as part of your professional brand.

- You have identified possible areas of weakness and have started to plan how to address these areas in preparation for your job hunt.
- You have begun to do research to identify opportunities that you can take advantage of and possible threats that could impede your success.
- You have identified professors or other knowledgeable professionals to serve as mentors.

Once you have done your own SWOT analysis, you can move forward to start making choices that reflect your strengths and interests.

CHAPTER 2

Career Choices: Get Curious, Take Initiative

The trouble is, if you don't risk anything, you risk even more.

—Erica Jong

Many students (not just communicators) don't have a clue what they want to do professionally when they start out. Even if you *think* you know what you are destined to do, chances are you will wind up doing something different from what you had envisioned during college. Perhaps several different things.

Choosing a career direction is exciting, even if a bit daunting. As a marketing communications major, you already have a career direction, and you may even be inspired to work for a particular industry, such as sports, beauty, music, or health care, for example. That's a great place to start as you consider your options, but don't let that be *all* you consider.

Perspectives: Esraa Elzin, Influencer + Social Lead, Brand Marketing, Instacart

Having worked for start-ups, agencies, and in-house for several companies, I recommend starting at a marketing communications agency, preferably as an intern. You learn from the ground up. It's a lot of work, especially because some tasks are tedious when you start out. In beauty PR, you may manage the sample closet and send samples to influencers. You learn to be super nimble because so much is thrown at you, such as managing time, setting priorities, working with client budgets, and communicating effectively with sometimes-demanding clients.

Beyond my assigned work, what mattered was the client's success and satisfaction because the agency's success depends on it. There's a lot of pressure, hard work, and long hours. It can sometimes feel make or break, but it's worth it! You learn a lot of new skills, grow your confidence, and become a stronger professional.

Working at an agency also helped grow my interests. When I started, I was assigned to clients in whom I had little interest, but I learned so much about how different brands are structured that I found myself enjoying the work.

Moving in-house was easy after working at an agency because agency training helps you understand brand management. When you're in-house, you determine how best to communicate your brand to your stakeholders. It's your decision to support or dismiss ideas because you know your brand values and customers the best. You may even find yourself managing the relationship with a media agency.

It's common for students to feel anxious or confused about having to narrow their choices when they start out. This is especially true for marketing communications majors because there are so many internship and career opportunities: advertising management, strategy, planning, creative, production, media buying, digital content or search engine optimization/search engine marketing (SEO/SEM), media relations, corporate PR, social media/influencer marketing, artificial intelligence (AI), user experience (UX), and many other areas, as the field evolves. You can also choose to work for marketing, digital, PR, advertising, or media agencies ranging from smaller boutique firms to global multinational agencies, corporations or small businesses, not-for-profits (local, national, or international), government agencies, nongovernmental organizations (NGOs), or start-ups. That's a lot to choose from.

Perspectives: Anne Tan-Detchkov, Director of Communications & Marketing, Project for Public Spaces

During college, I was curious about PR careers for nonprofits and mission-driven work compared to PR for products, consumer campaigns, or corporations. I interned with several consumer PR agencies, which led to getting hired. I learned a lot working for agencies. I felt challenged to bring smart, creative work that clients valued and to be accountable for results. It was a great foundation for my career.

After several years, I started thinking about whether my work genuinely aligned with my values. Even though I was successful, it felt unsatisfying. After serious reflection, I decided I would be happier working for a nonprofit whose mission aligned better with my values.

While agency work gave me excellent training, I liked the not-for-profit culture better. I felt less pressured, even though I put in long hours. Working with colleagues, donors, volunteers, and other stakeholders was more collaborative, because we were working for a mission we cared about.

One big challenge is working with limited budgets and staffing. You have to do more with less, while being creative and resourceful to deliver great work. It takes being scrappy. I taught myself a lot of new skills and wear many hats: media relations, website and social media content, graphic design, direct mail, publications, and photography. I feel lucky to use my communication skills for organizations that affect people's lives in important ways that matter to me.

Careers Are a Jungle Gym

Allow me to take some pressure off you, starting now.

It's okay if you don't know what you want to do professionally for the rest of your life. It's even okay if you are not certain about what kind of internship to take. But you do need to start somewhere! If you are not certain which direction to go, just try something.

On the other hand, if you are passionate about working in a particular industry, such as fashion, entertainment, or sports (popular among many students), of course look for opportunities to gain experience in these areas, but keep in mind that these jobs are highly competitive. You'll have to really stand out and perhaps work harder and smarter to get your foot in the door.

Follow your dreams, but use this time to also explore industries where there may be greater demand, such as in pharmaceuticals, technology, business, and financial sectors. These sectors may also offer higher starting salaries, compared to other industries. You are more likely to land a job if you cast a wider net.

In her book *Lean In*,[1] Sheryl Sandberg quotes Pattie Sellers, CEO, Sellers | Easton, who said, "Careers are a jungle gym, not a ladder." While the "career ladder" metaphor sets you on a defined, linear upward path, the jungle gym metaphor expands options and gives you permission to go in different directions and to try out stuff that you had not considered. College is the ideal time to take advantage of this exploration by doing several diverse internships and getting other professional experience. This is your time to experiment.

I picture a career path as an upward, expandable spiral. As you gain experience, you move up in rank and responsibility, but you can also expand and build on your strengths and experiences in new ways, so you are not so locked in to the same job. There is room to grow in other ways, too. Your career can expand, shift, and morph, as you do. Where you start does not have to limit where you end up. The important thing is to just get on the spiral.

At some point, if you want to transition to another profession such as health care, education, or law, as some of my students have done, you will have a superb foundation to change professions because of your strong communication skills which are needed in virtually every industry.

> ### Perspectives: Domonique Chaplin, MS, Public and Media Relations Manager, NYU Langone Health
>
> The journey from the start of your academic career to where you end up working is hardly ever linear.
>
> I was always interested in health care. But finding where I fit in the industry took time. I began studying nursing as an undergraduate, only to realize that patient care was not for me. My adviser recommended health care communications—and that advice proved pivotal.
>
> As a communications major, my first PR internship was with a national suicide prevention organization. The experience gained from that opportunity prepared me for my next internship turned full-time job in the bioscience division of a global PR agency. Continuing to build on that experience, I worked in-house for a communications consultancy, followed by a hospital, and later a pharmaceutical company.
>
> Communications has been a great way to diversify my professional experience by working in the agency, in-house, and nonprofit environments. The growth gained and insights learned from each role has brought me to my current passion: community health.

While writing this book, I have reflected on my own journey. In college, I envisioned myself having a career in music. But as I came to terms with my own limitations, I had to make other choices about my career. As an arts administration graduate student, I never planned to do public relations professionally. But good job opportunities in public relations came along that excited me, despite not being on my radar.

Being open to opportunities worked for me to jump-start my communications career. In grad school, I learned about a volunteer opportunity as a manager for the local community orchestra. I had to teach myself everything on the job, including doing publicity, so I took a book on how to write a press release out of the library. (My first intro to PR!) I got my first full-time job in PR by attending the American Symphony Orchestra League Convention (now the League of American

Orchestras), where I met an executive from a classical artist management agency who liked my experience and offered me the publicist job on the spot. I didn't plan on it, but my PR career took off from there. I built a career in both rewarding and unexpected ways.

Life and careers happen in ways that are wonderfully—and unfortunately—sometimes painfully unexpected. There is no "one size fits all guaranteed approach to success" when you start your career. That fact is liberating but also scary. What's important is to start somewhere and get experience.

Perspectives: Tasha Gilroy, Global Chief Belonging Officer, VML

While most young professionals enter the agency world with marketing communications majors, agencies also look for professionals with varied backgrounds and degrees such as psychology or computer engineering to work with clients in related disciplines. There are lots of opportunities for professionals who want to pivot to a communications career.

Working for a global agency that's part of a holding company, such as VML, which is part of WPP, enables new professionals to explore many different career paths. Holding companies have huge global clients shared across many operating companies. You're not limited only to your specific team and agency. You may work with professionals at sibling agencies on special projects or pro bono work, or on international projects where you are part of a global team. Early on, you get expertise and exposure to people at very high levels. This opens so many possibilities.

Another benefit is that moving to a sibling agency within the holding company can open even more career options. If you start at one WPP agency and move to another, your employment "start date" remains fixed at the date you started with the first WPP agency, which allows you to maximize your experience. This also benefits

employees who want to expand their careers in new ways at different
agencies within the holding company.

Get Curious: Get in the Driver's Seat

Overseeing internships for CCNY's communications department, I
often had students drop by my office to ask if I "knew of any internships
for them." While I applauded them for being proactive and asking for
guidance, helping them was especially challenging if they had not done
research or had not thought about what they were interested in. If they
told me, "I'm open for anything," they had even more work to do,
because *they* were the ones who needed to make choices based on their
abilities and interests. By taking no initiative and being passive, they had
inadvertently taken a back seat in their own career launch, which is a
weak place to start.

Here are a few steps you can take to jump start your initiative:

Start with your SWOT analysis from Chapter 1. Ask yourself what
types of careers would be a match for your strengths and interests.
Most communications jobs require research, good writing, and
analytical skills. Do you enjoy using a particular skill set, such as
research, writing, or analytics? Each takes you to a different role in
the industry.

Are you interested in a specific industry? Find out which agencies handle the communications for those companies. O'Dwyer's[2] lists agencies according to specialty clients, a great way to
target agencies that service clients in industries that fit with your
interests.

*Research internships on LinkedIn or Indeed, or do a Google
search for internships in your area.* You can also look at
volunteer opportunities and freelance communications jobs for
small start-ups as ways to get experience.

Dig deeper into your favorite brand on social media. Find out
which agency does their PR or advertising. Follow them on

LinkedIn and connect with their HR pros to show your interest and to learn more.

Visit your department's professional adviser to learn about internships, opportunities, and relationships you could benefit from.

Don't overlook your campus professional career counselors. You may discover opportunities and internships that you had not even considered. These counselors can be a great resource for helping you develop a strong resume and cover letter.

Talk to other students who might have had internships so you can learn about opportunities that are great and avoid those that are not so great.

Perspectives: Heather Lynn Burnside, Performance Media Analyst, Spark Foundry

From my experience, when opportunities reveal themselves, take the initiative. Don't second guess yourself. If you think you don't deserve or don't have the abilities to accept them, remember the hardships you've overcome and why you overcame them. Always learn from the past, look forward to the future.

After earning my bachelor's degree in liberal arts I had a tough time finding work because of an economic recession. I supported myself in a variety of jobs doing data entry, office administration, customer service, and working part-time as a manager for a community garden on Chicago's South Side.

In June 2021, the COOP Careers program found my LinkedIn profile and shared information about how to apply. After learning about COOP's mission to train underemployed professionals and helping them transition into digital marketing and data analytics (and other areas), I applied because I was interested in social media and how businesses use it to build customer relationships. I saw this as an opportunity to improve my skills and my chances of finding better employment. After rounds of interviews, I was so excited to be accepted into COOP's four-month digital marketing program. I benefitted greatly from the support of my team "pod" and mentorship from COOP's instructors. I learned digital analytic skills and obtained multiple certifications to boost my credentials, in addition to taking advantage of COOP's networking opportunities and professional development and guidance resources.

Through the program, I met Spark Foundry's recruiters at a Google Talent Match and got a job without an internship because they saw the value of my work experience and the skills I learned through COOP. The recruiters were also impressed by my determination, grit, and support of others. Since joining Spark Foundry, I've worked on multiple client accounts with a talented team. There have been many challenges to overcome, but I'm grateful to have a supervisor and colleagues who have been supportive, sympathetic, and encouraging. Even though the work can be pressured and fast-paced, I am constantly learning. It's a matter of constantly expanding myself and adapting to client needs on tight deadlines. I make a point to remember the successes I have achieved at work and in life, along with learning valuable lessons from my failures. Most of all, I try to give myself grace and remind myself that I am doing my best.

Be Open to Other Opportunities

Stay on the lookout if your department or college hosts a panel discussion with business or industry leaders or if there is an industry event that you can attend in your area. You can maximize this experience by introducing yourself to the speaker after the event, telling them what you appreciated about their contributions and by asking for their business card to follow up. This shows that you are motivated to reach out to them, and, even if not in the immediate future, it's a record should you ever want to connect again. (See Chapter 4.) Even better, share your own business card so an interested contact can follow up with you if you make a great impression. (See Chapter 6.) I have students who landed great internships and jobs this way.

Second Languages Boost Your Options

If you are bilingual, there are potentially many more opportunities that can give you an edge in career options. As U.S.-based businesses increasingly target multicultural audiences, strong Spanish communicators, for example, are in greater demand. If you are strong in French, German, Italian, Spanish, or Portuguese, you may be competitive for an in-house corporate or marketing communications role for multinational businesses, or with global agencies that have international clients that could benefit from your language expertise and strategic communication skills.

One of my former students who was bilingual in Portuguese landed her entry-level dream job at a leading global PR agency whose clients were sponsors at the Olympic Games Rio 2016 in her home country, Brazil. Her language skills, coupled with her communications savvy, made her an ideal fit for the job and helped to launch her career in international public relations across a range of sports properties and events.

Perspectives: Erika Sanchez, Cofounder, Braid Communications; President, New York Chapter, Hispanic Public Relations Association (HPRA)

Being bilingual, especially in Spanish, is a huge asset for a communicator. When you are part of two cultures, you bring important understanding of both American and Hispanic Latino cultures, not only in the United States but also abroad. It opens opportunities, if you want to work globally.

I started my own agency a few years ago after having worked for agencies representing general market clients after graduation. I had always dreamed of being my own boss. Now, with my own agency, I enjoy working with mostly women clients and Hispanic businesses, so I can use my professional know-how in ways that mean the most to me personally.

Joining a professional industry organization is key for students and especially for recent grads. HPRA chapters in New York, Miami, Texas, and Los Angeles support students through scholarships, mentoring, and networking and panel events held in-person and online. The New York Chapter's leadership committee works closely with the board and is open to students and recent grads so that young pros can integrate into the organization early on and gain important leadership skills.

Show Up at Industry Events and Seminars

As the filmmaker Woody Allen is famously quoted as having said, "Eighty percent of success in life is showing up." This is certainly true for students who want to break into the marketing communications business.

Attending professional networking seminars and even informal industry meetups is one of the most important ways to build your network. Showing up sends a powerful message that you see yourself as a professional and are serious about connecting with other professionals for internships and job opportunities. Showing up at industry events puts you in touch with a targeted group of professionals who want to meet outstanding prospective interns or hires and to help students. This is your chance to make a strong in-person impression that could lead to significant opportunities. But if you don't go you miss out.

Annual events like Where Are All the Black People (WAATBP), sponsored by The One Club in New York, is an example of a networking event to mentor and recruit diverse talent. The annual multiday fall event attracts C-suite advertising industry leaders, senior professionals, and students to talk about the industry, build community, network, and hone professional skills. While face-to-face encounters are generally more powerful, some seminars are virtual, so students can attend even if they are not in the New York Metro area. Every effort to network counts because you never know whom you will meet.

Other industry events, like the Public Relations Student Society of America (PRSSA), which hosts its own multiday program at the Public

Relations Society of America (PRSA)'s annual conference, is another great way to network and build skills.

Perspectives: Genesis Flores, Production Coordinator, Music Industry

I went to a few PRSSA and AAF club events because I was curious. I learned the value of networking early on because I met an alumna who later hired me as an intern for her agency and who is still a mentor! I got excited about marketing communications and saw that this major could help me achieve my goals.

I took a lot of initiative as a student to set myself up for a job when I graduated. I joined CCNY PRSSA's chapter and became president. This gave me leadership experience running events and networking with professionals. Plus my involvement showed prospective employers that I was a committed student. I found professors who would mentor me outside of class. Despite getting tough feedback on my resume, I learned how to be more competitive and how to take constructive feedback even if it bruised my ego.

Because I wanted to do everything possible to secure a job when I graduated, I applied and was accepted to the IRTS Foundation and the 4A's MAIP summer internship programs. Both were great for building an industry network, and I got important experience and professional training, plus an entry into two internships that jump-started my career.

Even before I chose marketing communications as my major, I had a big choice: use my education for what I wanted to do, or fulfill my parents' dreams for me. As immigrants, my parents wanted to see me in a high-paying job like a doctor. After one semester, I realized that premed was not a good fit. I was excited about doing advertising or PR in the entertainment industry. Because I paid for my own education, I chose the path I wanted.

Don't Let Fear of Rejection Stop You From Trying

Applying for an internship or job can feel like a monumental effort. Unfortunately, fear of rejection or even the fear of making "a wrong choice" can cause some students to take *no* action and to wait for something to come along on its own. Not applying to anything is worse than taking thoughtful steps to apply to *something* to start getting experience, even if it's not perfect. Or, as one of my mentors advised, "Even if you don't *'know'* for sure what path to take, don't say *'no'* to opportunities out of uncertainty or fear of trying."

Everyone experiences rejection at some point. While it doesn't feel good, it's important to start building your resilience now. You'll need it for the long term. The only way to do this is to keep trying and keep applying. If you get rejected, look for the next opportunity.

If you are rejected from every internship you apply for, there is always a Plan B. Look for volunteer opportunities in communications with community organizations that might need help with their communications, or consider asking if you can shadow a professional for a short period.

Getting exposure to a variety of jobs, industries, and work environments is a great way to begin to define the kind of career and workplace that best suits you. You have to start somewhere. Take the first step.

Perspectives: Ari Berkowitz, Social Strategy Director, Deloitte Digital

Besides interning in PR, media buying, and digital advertising agencies, doing freelance work for clients was a valuable resume builder during college. Prospective employers respect freelance experience because it shows a certain drive, ambition, and entrepreneurship that internships may not require.

Freelancing uses your abilities differently. As a paid freelancer, your employer expects you to problem solve to help their business. There is less hand-holding than with internships. Having to rely on my know-how and initiative built my confidence and experience, especially after I had freelanced for several clients. I learned a lot in the process. Once I had experience, I continued to take other freelance jobs that I learned about through my network and referrals. You have to be open to opportunities. They are out there.

My first freelance assignment, which I learned about from my professor, was for a local not-for-profit organization that needed to build their online social media presence for outreach and fundraising. Like most communications students, I was proficient in social media through my own usage. I could bring a lot of value for less money than the organization would have to pay an established professional.

While I did get paid for my work, income was not the main reason to freelance. The real value came from being completely responsible for my contributions, from the satisfaction I got from helping clients and from the experience I gained. In job interviews, my freelance experience was a great way to show prospective employers my initiative, problem-solving ability, and creativity to drive results. It helped get my foot in the door.

Chapter Wrap Up

- You have reviewed your brand SWOT analysis in terms of internships / jobs that are of interest to you to see where you might be excited to start working.
- You have done research to gather a list of options for internships that suit your strengths and interests.
- You have gone to other professionals on campus to learn about opportunities you may have not considered.
- You are committed to applying for opportunities, even if they are not perfect.
- You do not let rejection, even if painful, stop you from moving forward.

CHAPTER 3

Internships and Volunteerism: Getting Started

Experience is the best teacher.

—Attributed to Julius Caesar

If you plan to pursue a career in advertising, public relations, digital marketing, or another related field, taking at least one internship, preferably two or three, is *essential* to be competitive for the job market. Internships show that you are a serious young professional with the passion, professionalism, maturity, and knowledge to be successful in the workplace. You will gain valuable experience that employers look for when they hire, and interning gives you the opportunity to talk about your strengths and successes when you apply for jobs, and to showcase your skills working with clients and on teams. Additionally, internships give you important insights into the realities and challenges of the workplace to help build confidence and to be a competitive candidate when you apply for your first full-time job.

Internships also serve as a bridge between the classroom and the professional world. They help your development in four important ways: (1) They are a catalyst to build your professional resume; (2) they enable you to apply your studies to the workplace; (3) they help you discover the type of work and work environment that best suits you, and likewise, the kind of jobs and work environments that are not a good fit; and (4) they help you develop important social and professional skills working with supervisors, clients, and co-workers.

If you are uncertain about the kind of internship you want, it's still important to apply for opportunities that might appeal to you, even if not for the long run. This experience may put you on the path to identify the kind of work you are really excited about, or it might help you redirect your focus away from work that is unappealing or not a good fit for your skills and interests.

My daughter, a college English major, was uncertain about what career path to pursue after she graduated from college. I suggested she try interning with a PR agency, where she could use her strong research and writing skills. After taking two PR agency internships, one in business and technology, and another with medical/pharmaceutical clients, she concluded that public relations was *not* a good fit for her. But, based on the clients she worked with and her foray into media relations, she figured out that she really wanted to be journalist specializing in science. Or as she says, "I learned that I didn't want to be the PR person pitching the story, I wanted to be the reporter who PR people pitched stories to." That set her on her career path as a science journalist. Maybe she would have found that direction some other way, but these internships helped her to crystallize her strengths and passions while also helping her affirm what she did not want to do.

Perspectives: Genesis Flores, Production Coordinator, Music Industry

I applied to about 60 internships before landing at a global advertising agency as a broadcast production intern. Despite not having production classes, I had picked up some core skills up on my own. I had made a film for the MAIP intern program that showed my creativity.

I took on a lot of tasks that just needed to be done, asked a lot of questions, and learned the industry jargon. No one really has the time to teach you everything about how to do your job. Agency life moves fast, things are hectic, and everyone is busy, so you just have to figure things out for yourself.

When my internship ended, I dropped a lot of hints to my supervisor about continuing in a full-time role. This was during Covid, so no one was in the office. What made the difference was going to the office on a day that the head of production would be there. I introduced myself and told her exactly where I saw myself fitting in and made my pitch to get hired. She offered me a job on the last day of my internship.

Perfection Is the Enemy of the Good: Don't Let Uncertainty Stop You From Applying

Some students I worked with avoided applying for any internships because they couldn't decide what type of internship they wanted or were afraid of getting stuck on a track they didn't like. As a result, they didn't take any internships and missed out on important experience before graduating. This put them at a huge disadvantage when they were applying for jobs, since other competitive graduates had experience they lacked. Many were left feeling in limbo because internships are often harder to find after you have graduated.

Other students were afraid of applying for internships because they felt insecure and feared that they were not competitive. They took themselves out of the running to avoid risking rejection.

While no one enjoys rejection, experiencing it, learning from it, and moving on, are among the most important lessons you can learn from this process. You'll probably be going through this when you apply for jobs, so you may as well start to build your emotional resilience muscle now. And the only way to do that is to take strategic risks and to risk rejection.

Internship Options

There are several ways to take an internship, depending on your professional interests, your available time, your financial needs, and the time of year you are seeking to intern. Just remember, no one size fits all. You have the opportunity to explore and try working in a variety of industry roles and work environments.

Since many students hold down part-time jobs while attending college, it may be challenging to sacrifice earnings in place of an internship that may not pay as much or may not pay at all.

As a result, students will have to balance their priorities to determine if it is worthwhile for them to sacrifice earnings for important professional experience. It sometimes can be a difficult choice, but it is important to weigh all options, especially if you are trying to be competitive for your chosen career and you know that you need rudimentary marketing communications experience.

For most students who want to pursue a career in marketing communications, starting out interning at a marketing communications agency, whether in PR, advertising, or digital marketing, will probably give you the strongest foundation to build your career.

This is because you are working for a dedicated business that provides full-service support and counsel to clients. You will learn from and be surrounded by top communications professionals with a variety of expertise and will be exposed to a high level of thinking and strategy that you may not find working in-house for an organization.

Most agencies will not hire professionals without agency experience because the demands of servicing multiple clients and understanding an agency business model is a specialized expertise that you can only learn by working in that environment. So getting your foot in the door as a student intern with an agency is the best way in.

Thinking about your career progression, it generally is easier to transition from an agency to a business or enterprise, than it is to transition from a business to an agency. So think carefully about whether you want to build your career on an agency foundation, or if working in the nonprofit or government sectors, or others, might suit you better.

Paid Internships

Agencies

The most competitive internships are those offered by the major marketing communications agencies and national and international corporations / businesses. These are full-time, paid summer internship programs (8 to 10 weeks) for competitive college seniors (sometimes juniors), and can serve as a possible gateway to entry-level jobs. Interns generally are assigned a role on an agency team doing entry-level tasks, and may participate in agency-run professional development seminars and social activities. Many agencies place interns into teams and assign a client for whom they will create a strategic plan and do a simulated client pitch presentation before agency professionals.

Students should start applying for agency summer internships during the *prior* fall semester (i.e., six to nine months or so ahead of time) and into *early spring*, as most close out by March. Agencies will post internships on a dedicated link on their websites for students to apply. Students should apply to multiple opportunities (at least 20), since these are highly competitive.

By law, if an internship is paid, you are not required to take it for academic credit, which means registering and paying tuition for it as you would a class. However, some students may choose to take paid internships for academic credit anyway.

To allow students to take competitive but unpaid internships, such as with not-for-profit organizations, some colleges have designated funds to pay students for these experiences, if the sposoring organization does not offer a stipend. It's a good idea to ask your college career office if they offer such a program.

Businesses, Start-Ups, and Not-for-Profit Organizations

Perhaps you are interested in working in a particular market sector such as fashion, sports, health care, media, technology or the environment, or even for a social service organization or government agency. In that case, internships are a great way to get your foot in the door. Do some research on businesses and organizations that offer internships that intersect with your passions. Many have formal intern programs, mostly in the summer, but some might have options during the academic year.

Perspectives: Susan Akinyi-Tindi, Account Director, Dieste Health

Internships really shaped my career direction. As an international student, the stakes were higher if I didn't succeed. My dream was finding an employer who would sponsor my immigration visa, a huge hurdle.

My first internship with a PR agency was one of the best and worst experiences. Getting a competitive internship was a big motivator and validated my competitiveness. But I faced real challenges. Some supervisors don't give you clear direction and support you, even if you're supposed to be learning. Co-workers also may not have time to help or support you. I felt harshly judged, but I gained a better understanding of my strengths and weaknesses, and decided to try another internship in advertising.

My second internship in ad agency account management was great. It's a cliché that the people you work with make the difference but it's true! My manager was patient and kind, and helped me transition from intern to full-time. She had my back. To get hired, I had to stand out among 60 other interns by showing that my skills were relevant and valuable. My team supported me for a second internship. And I realized my dream! I got hired full-time and was sponsored for my immigration visa.

Local businesses and community organizations can also benefit from your marketing communications experience. If you are social media savvy, for example, interning with a local organization allows you to apply your skills to extend a business's social media reach and impact. This kind of experience is an ideal way to showcase your strategic thinking and creativity and to demonstrate that you are results-driven.

Nonpaid, For-Credit Internships

While many internships pay students by the hour or offer some kind of stipend, others do not. Both can offer value by way of helping students to gain experience. If an internship is paid, make sure you know in advance the hourly wage or stipend, the duration of the internship, and hours you are expected to work, and whether it is remote, on-site, or a combination. Also, make sure you have an on-site supervisor who is experienced and who can assign work and evaluate it, and who is available to you if you have questions.

If an internship is not paid, by law, students are required to register with their college for academic credit (see #3 in the following list). That means that the student works for free, *and* pays the college for course academic credit based on their work experience. This requires having a faculty member who can monitor the internship, evaluate the student's performance, and advocate for the student if issues arise. If you take an internship for academic credit, there will likely be academic guidelines as to how many hours you'll have to work and what assignments you'll have to complete for a grade. Your faculty should be able to give you guidance.

Students are more likely to find nonpaid internships during the academic year, in addition to summers, so this is a great opportunity to get experience and earn college credit.

Not all colleges offer internships for academic credit, so seek out that information from your college or university in advance.

To protect students against unfair labor practices, and to protect full-time employees, the U.S. Department of Labor has seven criteria for unpaid internships,[1] as follows:

1. The extent to which the intern and the employer clearly understand that there is no expectation of compensation. Any promise of compensation, express or implied, suggests that the intern is an employee—and vice versa.
2. The extent to which the internship provides training that would be similar to that which would be given in an educational environment, including the clinical and other hands-on training provided by educational institutions.
3. The extent to which the internship is tied to the intern's formal education program by integrated coursework or the receipt of academic credit.

4. The extent to which the internship accommodates the intern's academic commitments by corresponding to the academic calendar.

5. The extent to which the internship's duration is limited to the period in which the internship provides the intern with beneficial learning.

6. The extent to which the intern's work complements, rather than displaces, the work of paid employees while providing significant educational benefits to the intern.

7. The extent to which the intern and the employer understand that the internship is conducted without entitlement to a paid job at the conclusion of the internship.

Red Flags

If an unpaid internship does not list a supervisor and does not include a clear organizational mission and an outline of intern responsibilities, it's best to pass on it, since this is an indication that the sponsoring organization is not prepared to host a student for a viable educational experience. They may just be looking for free labor.

Do your homework before you sign on, or ask a faculty member familiar with internships in your field to help you vet the experience. Otherwise, you risk wasting your time working for people who are unprofessional and who will not provide appropriate guidance and instruction. In fact, some organizations will bring on students under the guise of internships to do their marketing for no charge, but provide no supervisory expertise to guide the student. My advice is to avoid these situations, which generally offer little substantive value.

Kezia Kent, Senior, The City College of New York, Double Major: Economics, Advertising/PR; Intern, The TASC Group

As I considered where to intern, it was important to find an opportunity that aligned with my interests and values. I considered the entertainment and beauty industries. However, because of my interest in social movement and climate change, I looked for organizations whose interests and clients that focused in these areas.

When interviewing, ask detailed questions about the company and the job to see if the company's values really reflect what they say in the job description. If an internship is not a good fit with your values, it's better to find out before you accept. In one situation, I shared constructive feedback with the interviewer that I found the job description misleading, which she appreciated. I also connected with her on LinkedIn because I know I can learn a lot from her. Even though the job did not work out, I made a great contact.

Where to Find Internships

Internships can be found at marketing communications agencies, businesses, corporations, nonprofits government agencies, or at start-ups, many of which need help with their marketing communications and digital presence. If you have a specific interest in an industry, such as sports, or beauty, or the environment, it's a great idea to research agencies and organizations with intern programs that could enhance your experience in these areas. For example, most of the major publishing houses and media businesses have summer publicity internships. Here are some specific resources:

- Meet with the professor in your department who oversees internships to determine your interests, opportunities, and the next steps to prepare to apply.
- Meet with the professionals in your campus career office and look at university postings. Many college career offices provide students with support in developing their cover letters, resumes, and LinkedIn profiles.
- Google search "internships" in your area/specialty.
- Do searches on SimplyHired, Indeed, or Mediabistro.

- Here is a partial list of industry sites that list marketing communication agencies (see Appendix for a list of these webpage links fully spelled out):
  - PR News & PR Firm Rankings | O'Dwyer's (odwyerpr.com)
  - Top Advertising Agencies in the United States (www.goodfirms.co)
  - The 30 Best Digital Advertising Agencies (www.webdesignrankings.com)
  - The Ultimate List of Agency Holding Companies & Their Affiliates (www.winmo.com)

Dedicated Internship Programs to Support Multicultural Students in Marketing Communications

There are several organizations that sponsor highly competitive paid summer internship programs with leading agencies to support diversity in the marketing communications industries (see Appendix for more). Among them are:

- Multicultural Internship Program (MAIP), sponsored by 4A's (American Association of Advertising Agencies)
- LAGRANT Foundation
- Emma Bowen Foundation
- T. Howard Foundation
- IRTS Foundation
- AdColor Futures
- New York Women in Communications
- AdFellows
- Marcus Graham Project

All have separate application processes that are generally posted in the fall of the year before the year the internship is offered. Applications require time and thought, so leave plenty of time to complete them.

Work Experience and Volunteerism Counts

If you have work experience, such as a waitperson, sales associate, office worker, delivery person, or other jobs that students frequently take, this also works to your advantage. It shows prospective internship employers that you are responsible, can deal with workplace demands, and are motivated to work. So do not underestimate the value of your experience. Make sure to include your other work experience when you are crafting your resume. Try to showcase results and value from your work.

If you do not have work experience, that is okay, too. Use your related classes to demonstrate your commitment to pursuing your profession and to showcase your foundational knowledge in your chosen area. Remember to look for opportunities to volunteer and to highlight your drive and professionalism.

Here are some opportunities to get experience that are not formal internships:

- **Volunteer for a campus student club in a leadership role** where you can demonstrate tangible outcomes from your work, such as increased enrollment in club members or attendance at club events, or increased social media followers based on content or events you create.
- **Join your local PRSSA or AAF chapter** to demonstrate your professionalism. A lot of agencies give priority to professional student club members in their internship hiring. Even better, run for a leadership position.
- **Volunteer for a community or religious organization** to apply your strong communication skills to help them achieve their mission and objective. This could include updating content on their website, social media, or other platforms, or even producing video or blog content about their work or the people affiliated with them.

Developing Your Application Materials

When you are developing your resume and cover letter for your internship applications, refer to Chapter 6, which provides you with specific guidelines to develop your materials. Having a professional social media presence applies to interns, too.

Interns also need to be competitive on strategies to find good internships, interview strongly, and demonstrate on-the-job professionalism, so Chapters 5 and 7 can be helpful at this stage as well.

Perspectives: Ibrahim Tatlicioglu, Media Planning Supervisor, EssenceMediacom

Learning how to be a good intern is kind of a beast. You have to be a little scrappy, you can't just wait around for people to tell you what to do or you risk being invisible. I was accepted to an internship in account management as part of VMLY&R's summer program, and was invited to continue my internship during the academic year, which is unusual. No one on my team expected to have interns, so I approached my internship always thinking about how I could add value. That was one reason I was invited to stay on.

You have to dig in and find ways to squeeze yourself into the workstream. I asked my team and supervisors about everything they were doing. I looked at other people's calendars and asked, "What's this meeting? Can I join?"

I also looked for ways to make my boss's life easier. For example, I took the initiative to figure out how he wanted his meeting notes written up and always sent a recap note after every single meeting. If you take initiative and have a really good attitude around the office, your boss will remember it. It's not simple, but you just have to push yourself.

Learning how to ask questions in a productive way is one of the most important things you can do. When I started out, I asked a lot of general questions that sucked, based on how people responded to me. I realized that I needed to first do some homework on my own to figure out what exactly I needed to know, and then go back and give them some context. People are not mind readers and you need to tell them why you are asking and what you are trying to accomplish.

Negative Experiences Offer Value, Too

While everyone hopes for a great internship experience, this is not always the case. Some of the most important insights that shaped my career came from challenging internships (and jobs) that made me rethink the kind of work and environment I wanted, as much as what I did *not* want.

If your internship is not a great experience, you can still benefit. Reflect on what specifically caused you to feel the internship was not successful. There's a lot you can learn to help you through the next internship or even your first job:

- Did you learn something about a particular industry or workplace culture that showed it's not a good fit for your interests, skills or work style?
- Did you have challenges working effectively with a boss or on a team? If so, is there something you could do differently next time to be more effective? Or does the experience point to another type of environment or job that is better suited to you?
- Did you learn something about your own abilities to set priorities, multitask, take direction, deliver on deadline, and be an effective part of a team? If you felt that you were not at your best, is there something you want to change in your next work experience?

Perspectives: Mushfiqa Andalib—Bachelor of Arts, Communications, The City College of New York

I found my first internship with a lifestyle podcaster on Indeed.com. To be honest, it was a tough experience. I often felt like an imposter. Because this was my first internship, I didn't really feel prepared to deliver the kind of professional writing that I was assigned. Even though I was a strong student in class and was committed to understanding how I could improve, this was different. I had a lot of questions. I'd ask my supervisor for guidance, but I often felt like she was frustrated with my questions and the work I turned in.

Intern supervisors need to get their work out and don't always have the time to help interns. In my major coursework, I was used to getting clear feedback from professors on how I could improve my writing and thinking. At this internship, I was supposed to be learning from my supervisor, but ultimately, I was expected to figure most things out for myself.

My second internship with a small beauty PR agency was a much better experience because I had a clear set of responsibilities and knew my schedule and tasks. I got a better sense of what PR entails and I could deliver better work.

My supervisor was more understanding. While she too needed to get the work out, she also gave me much clearer feedback on what I needed to do differently to deliver better work so I would not make the same mistakes again. I'd rather have a supervisor tell me what I was doing wrong so I could fix it and feel good about contributing. You can't always know what kind of a person you are getting as a supervisor until you are working for them.

Chapter Wrap Up

- You have committed to finding and applying for at least one internship while you are in college, even if you are uncertain as to whether this is the perfect internship.
- You have reached out to your department faculty and your campus career office at least six months prior to your desired internship to ascertain internship descriptions, time of year offered, application deadlines, and requirements.

- You have conducted research to help you determine whether you want to intern with an agency or in-house with a business, start-up, not-for-profit or government agency.
- You have made a list of at least 20 places to apply.
- You have consulted Chapter 6 to begin to develop your resume and cover letters for your application.
- You have done your homework to find appropriate opportunities and understand that just because you apply does not mean you'll be accepted.

CHAPTER 4

Networking: Your BFF Starting Now

It's not just who you know, it's who knows you.

—Sam Rapkin (and others)

While your personal brand, strengths, and attributes may make you competitive for an internship or job, the network of people you create throughout your career is instrumental to your success beyond your own efforts.

Networking doesn't start when you get a job. It starts with your college peers, professors, and the professionals whom you meet. In fact, it could include customers you meet on your job, or even casually. You never know how the connection you form today will affect your life later.

Perspectives: Luis Herrera, Senior, The City College of New York, Advertising/PR Program; Sports Intern, Roc Nation; Influencer Marketing Intern, New York Giants

I started building my network in high school when I played basketball. I learned that knowing how to build good relationships in sports, like being a team player, is also important in public relations, which is a relationship-driven business.

I have met amazing mentors through school, my job, networking events, and internships who have been essential to my professional growth. As a bartender, two of my customers became mentors because I was curious about what they do and I let them see who I really am. One mentor, an NBA agent, saw my passion for sports and shared insights on the work it takes to be successful. Another mentor from my community was pivotal in helping me with my resume to land my first internship doing media relations for a college sports team. I listened to their advice, took their feedback, and put it into action.

My professors mentored me by sharing writing tips for my internship sports features, which I used in my portfolio and on LinkedIn. At Berk Communications, where I landed an internship through my PRSSA involvement on LinkedIn, I was lucky to have mentors and champions from co-workers up to executives. Even though I was nervous, they could see that I was excited to learn. They have become champions who have recommended me for other internships so I could keep growing.

One of the most important things I do is show my appreciation to mentors and to those who help me along the way. I send follow-up notes any time I have an interaction, or I post a positive experience on LinkedIn. I look for ways to turn disappointments into positives. When I didn't get selected for a big scholarship, I wrote to the sponsor to thank him for considering me. I was amazed when he wrote back that it was the first time he had received a letter like that and offered to help me in the future.

While finding great mentors has been crucial in my journey, believing in myself is also essential because it helps me to show my mentors that I have what it takes to earn their support.

During my years at CCNY, at the start of the semester when students were nervous about acclimating to new classes and people, I asked students to introduce themselves to the people sitting around them and urged them to grab a coffee with someone they may not have known well. Not just to be sociable, but because *you never know who you meet that will eventually affect your career,* whether by hiring you, sharing job openings, putting in a good word with the hiring team, or possibly even going into business together.

In my own career, networking was instrumental in being hired at three of my five jobs. Without my network, I would never even have heard of those opportunities, let alone get on the radar of the hiring team. In fact, people in my network *reached out to me* to share job openings without knowing I was job hunting. The dividends networking paid in my life included meeting my husband Joe, whom I was introduced to by a former work colleague from five years earlier, who tracked me down. That's why it matters who knows you, not just who you know!

Well into my career, growing my network was among the most important investments I made when I joined the CCNY faculty. I knew that professional contacts for CCNY's Advertising/PR program beyond the ones I already had were not only essential for *my* success, but even more important for my *students'* success. I joined the PRSA, became active in the New York PRSA chapter, and founded our PRSSA campus chapter. I also looked for ways to expand my network to advertising executives and HR recruiters for student internships and job networking. That amazing professional community opened doors for my students and contributed tremendously to my life, some becoming friends beyond the professional connection. Networking enriches our lives in ways we cannot imagine.

Take the Initiative to Connect: Business Cards Help to Pave the Way

Building your network while you're in college extends beyond your classmates and professors. Attending professional networking events, industry panel discussions and events, for example, is essential to build and expand your professional network.

If you meet someone with whom you want to follow up for an internship, job, or an informational interview to learn more about them and what they do, *ask for their business card*. Make a note on the card when you met them and any important details about the encounter. That way, you can send them a follow-up e-mail and remind them of your meeting and who you are (don't assume that people will remember you without some memory prompts). You can also send them a LinkedIn request to further solidify the connection.

Just as important, you should always carry your *own* business cards to share with professionals you meet. This is an essential professional tool for all business professionals. Others may be equally inspired to reach out to you to share job opportunities, and you do not want them to have to rely on their memory to guess how to spell your name or why they want to stay in touch (see Chapter 6 for more on business cards). If you want to affirm your genuine interest in building a connection, take the initiative and offer them your card telling them how much you enjoyed meeting them and that you'd like to stay in touch. They will ideally make their own positive notes about you on your card to help them remember who you are, too.

Business cards are not only valuable in the short term, they can be an important way to get back in touch with someone even after time has passed. Your professional credentials will change faster than you realize. You never know how someone you meet can be an important contact years later. Create a dedicated system and place to keep your business cards, including digitally, so you can build on your network over time and you don't lose valuable contacts. Having an orderly contact file is still essential.

It Starts With Personal Relations

One of the most important lessons I shared in my public relations classes was that all good *public* relations starts with good *personal* relations. Positive personal relations impact every aspect of your life: being a productive and positive team member in your agency, connecting with your boss and senior management; interacting with clients, the media, and vendors; networking with other professionals at events; and even how you connect to people in your nonwork life. You never know how someone can affect your career and life, or how you can impact theirs.

Terrie Williams, founder of The Terrie Williams Agency, the first Black female-owned PR agency, devoted pages of her timeless and inspiring book *The Personal Touch*[1] to highlighting how she built relationships that impacted her life in profound ways, whether it was connecting with luminaries who became her clients, or by being a good member of her community and society by showing concern and consideration for others. Beyond offering an extraordinary account of her own story, she offers great tangible tips that anyone can use.

Linda Kaplan Thaler, another industry icon, founder of the Kaplan Thaler Agency, wrote about the importance of personal connections in her book *The Power of Nice: How to Conquer the Business World with Kindness*[2] with Robin Koval. Like Terrie Williams, she offers tangible examples and tips showing how relating to others with kindness contributed to her career and life success. While she uses "nice" as a core value, I prefer the notion of being "gracious." "Nice" can be passive. "Graciousness" shows your active intent and appreciation.

As a student of communications, the importance of making connections with people is a no-brainer. Here are my ABCs for good personal relations:

- Be kind to everyone you meet.
- Be open to everyone you meet. They matter and have value. You never know how a chance meeting may lead to something bigger for you *or* them.
- Be an active listener. You do this by affirming what is being said to you and by following up with your own relevant observations or questions to their comments.
- True relationships are earned over time and do not happen through superficial connections. All relationships take nurturing, investment, and attention.
- Do not take connections for granted. Find time to invest and show gratitude.
- Don't make all your outreach transactional by looking for an immediate personal benefit.
- Reach out because you are genuinely interested in meeting someone, not just because you want them to do something for you.

- Always, always, *always* say thank you in writing (e-mail is okay, texting is not) to show appreciation when someone meets or talks with you to give advice. Be sincere and gracious.
- People in the communications field genuinely *like* helping other people! Don't be afraid to reach out to someone you want to meet on LinkedIn or at an event. But if you are going to do that, make sure you do your homework about them, so you know who you are connecting to and why you are reaching out.

My Favorite Thank You Note: A Parable

As a graduate student in arts administration, I took a six-month marketing internship with an orchestra as part of my degree requirements. While I had a great working relationship with the marketing director to whom I reported, throughout my time there the orchestra's managing director treated me in a dismissive and condescending manner. I felt demoralized and diminished.

As I wrapped up my stint there, I wanted to do something to get closure with the director. I did not feel that I could tell him what I honestly felt because I was not in a position of power, he probably wouldn't care and, therefore, the honest feedback would likely serve no purpose. Plus, I might have needed him again in the future as a reference, since the orchestra business is a small world.

My father, always a wise counsel, suggested I do the following: He told me to send the director flowers with a note that said "F--- you," but, he said, spell it "T-h-a-n-k y-o-u." I followed his advice. I got closure. I felt good because I knew what my real sentiments were behind the gesture. It didn't matter to me whether he knew my true feelings.

You never know when your paths may cross with someone again and whether they could impact your career in some way. When possible, it's better to leave on a positive note than a negative one. *Thank you* is always in style.

LinkedIn Is Your Networking Super Highway

Using LinkedIn proactively is one of the most important ways to build your network. It starts with creating a strong LinkedIn profile (see Chapter 7) that amplifies your professionalism and areas of interest, even just starting out.

Once you have a strong profile, you can reach out to HR professionals at agencies or businesses that interest you. You can find ways to connect with like-minded professionals through professional organizations, associations, and affinity groups.

Better than using LinkedIn's standard boilerplate invitation to connect, send a brief, personalized message about your interest in the company or person that shows you have done your homework and that your desire to connect is genuine. You can take this one step further by using LinkedIn messaging to request an informational interview with an HR pro or someone else at the company.

While you probably won't get positive responses from everyone you reach out to, if you are professional and targeted in your approach, this can be an important way to expand your professional contacts. LinkedIn also allows other professionals to find you, too, which becomes even more important as your career evolves. See the LinkedIn section of Chapter 6 for tips on building your LinkedIn profile.

Here are a few suggestions to make your LinkedIn networking more effective:

- Build your LinkedIn relationships. A cold outreach without first building a relationship is not the most effective way to connect with people you don't know, although it can work sometimes.
- Lay the groundwork for a relationship. Before reaching out, do your homework on the person you wish to connect to by reading their LinkedIn profile and noting areas that are of specific interest to you. That way when you write to them, you can say something about *them* that's of special interest to you. It shows them you have taken time to appreciate who they are professionally and that you value their time and interest.

- Follow the individual on LinkedIn first. Build a connection on their LinkedIn page by reading what they are posting. Add a comment about its value or interest to you. Repost their article on your LinkedIn with a comment. Engage with them on their LinkedIn turf to show that you are serious.
- If possible, get a warm referral. If you know someone who is connected to the person you want to reach, ask if you can use them as a reference for an introduction. Perhaps they will send a LinkedIn message with your profile making an introduction. Short of that, once you get approval to use their name, message the target person on LinkedIn telling them who you were referred by and ask for an opportunity to connect further.

Perspectives: Jerry Louis, Associate Creative Director, UnitedMasters/Translation

Networking is 90 percent of how you navigate and build your career in this industry. Networking starts in college—doing group projects, studying with other comms majors and bonding over classes. You'll meet fellow students over and over after graduation, so it's important to start making those connections early. I heard about my first agency internship from another comms major who had a great experience and encouraged me to apply. I also attended every networking event my program offered and participated in the 4A's MAIP program to build my connections to industry professionals.

During my project management internship at Saatchi and Saatchi, I realized I wanted to get into copywriting. Another intern and I took the initiative to collaborate on a creative portfolio of mock campaigns. That really helped launch my career as an advertising creative.

Your network and mentors will also help you stay the course when the going gets tough. Sometimes, staring at a blank page, I wonder, "Am I really creative?" When you feel that way, people in your network can help you push through your self-doubt.

During my 11 years in advertising, every job I got has been through a networking connection, including some from my undergraduate time at City College. People sometimes will reach out to share a job opening or I'll hear about opportunities at a conference. I once contacted an advertising professional at Weiden and Kennedy for career advice and got offered a job! Networking has been absolutely essential to my success.

Mentors, Advocates, and Champions

Mentors are powerful counselors and allies with whom you create a more substantive relationship. These are people (whether within your professional circle or not) whom you respect, trust, and value, and with whom you build a deeper connection to receive ongoing guidance, advice, and support, for either the short or the long term. Mentors can help you with immediate concerns by being a sounding board if you are struggling with a specific issue. Beyond this, however, they can help you to expand your thinking and inspire you to grow in ways you thought were beyond you. Plus, they can help to expand your network.

Not everyone in your network will play equal roles in your career path. Some people will be superficial contacts you meet as part of your broader professional experience and outreach. Other relationships can profoundly impact on your success. In my own life, mentors have been bosses, wise colleagues, friends, and professionals who believed in me, affirmed my value, and pushed me to go beyond what I thought I could do. They were invaluable to my personal and professional growth.

You can find mentors among your professors, alumni from your college, business professionals, affinity groups, even through your church or community. Ideally, it's helpful to work with someone with some understanding of the communications industry so they have context as to how to best advise you. It is within your power to ask someone if they would mentor you, so look around, see who you know and respect, or reach out to someone you admire and with whom you want to build a relationship. The ball, as they say, is in your court.

Unless someone expressly volunteers to mentor you through a designated professional program such as The LAGRANT Foundation or MAIP, it's important that you build a relationship with your mentor *before* you ask them to help you. This takes time and often requires that they have a sense of you personally and what your professional interests and capabilities are. For example, if you have a professor or adviser who you admire, it's reasonable to ask that person to mentor you because they have an idea of your capabilities from class. But asking a professor you never had or who does not know you is not your best choice for a mentor. While you may admire them, they probably know little or nothing about you. So, best to begin by building a relationship and helping them understand what you bring, and how your goals can sync with what they can offer.

Mentoring Is Give and Take

Mentors get pleasure in helping others. They take joy in their mentee's successes, and they take satisfaction in helping mentees address challenges. They give you their time and expertise, but you, as a mentee, also have a role to play to make this a productive partnership.

This starts by not taking the relationship for granted. If someone invests their time in you, your job is to show up for meetings and to come prepared with information to share. Even if it's just a "check in," be prepared to honestly share what is really going on, good or bad. Your mentor's main job is to serve as a sounding board and to provide counsel in your professional development.

Beyond receiving guidance, your job is to put their advice into practice, and to share feedback on your progress. You will get more out of the relationship by managing the relationship, rather than relying on your mentor to take the lead. That means setting up regular, ongoing meetings as mutually agreed upon, and preparing an agenda including action items that you want to discuss or questions you want to address.

Think about who you have in your sphere who might mentor you starting now. Start by asking to meet with them to discuss your short-term goals and how they can help you. Do not approach someone without having first thought about how you would like them to help you. After you meet with your mentor, always send a short note of thanks. E-mail is okay, text is not, unless they prefer text communications.

Remember to connect with them every few months, even if it's just a check-in to tell them what you are up to and to show your gratitude for their support. Make sure you contribute to the relationship besides receiving, even by simply asking how they are doing—and listening to the answer.

Advocates and Champions

While you can benefit from mentors at any stage of your career, especially starting out, advocates are of real value once you are in the workplace. They are generally professionals with whom you work, who will go to bat to help you in your career development and your growth within a company. As an intern, it may mean having members of your team advocate for you to be hired to a full-time post, which is a powerful way to transition into your first job. Later in your career, advocates can be powerful allies to help you get a raise or promotion, or to be included in a high-profile project.

Champions, like advocates, are generally senior leaders in your business who have power to affect your career by strongly advocating for your advancement. Even when you are an intern, champions can impact your being hired.

Chapter Wrap Up

- You have identified at least one person in your sphere who could serve as a mentor while you take your first steps to apply for internships or jobs.
- You commit to building this relationship by staying in touch regularly (to be determined by you and your mentor), and by showing your gratitude.
- You have created a strong LinkedIn profile to empower you to connect with others on LinkedIn and to help others find you.

CHAPTER 5

Get Your Game On: Your Strategic Plan

Hope is not a strategy.

—Attributed to Vince Lombardi

Landing a job is a marathon, not a sprint. Preparing to effectively showcase your professional self in job applications takes planning and time. Be prepared to dedicate several hours a week. It could take months to get to the finish line, getting hired, so do your best to stay fueled, mentally and physically.

If you are serious about finding a job, you'll need planning and endurance. This means you will want to be:

Proactive to move past your fear so you can go after the kind of job you want.

Organized in setting up a job file on your computer to track progress and monitor your outreach.

Disciplined to keep at it despite having other responsibilities or feeling discouraged.

Strategic in how you plan to build your network and where you apply.

Committed to investing time in the process on a regular basis, ideally, daily.

Thick-Skinned to accept constructive criticism, even if you feel bad.

Resilient to persevere despite not getting responses and being rejected.

Stay Motivated

Honestly, it's hard to keep putting out effort when you are not getting positive feedback, or when you are pulled in other directions with other responsibilities, not to mention needing some quality "you" time.

Everyone has ups and downs in their job search. At times you will feel like you're on a roller coaster and are at a low point. Here's a tip to help you through:

You may think you must be motivated to work better,

BUT…

Working better definitely helps your motivation!

Even when you are just "not feeling it," try these relatively simple suggestions:

Commit to doing something job-search related every day (or at least every other day.) Even when it's hard, spend a minimum of 30 minutes working on your plan, checking LinkedIn or Indeed or elsewhere for job openings, researching a company you may not have considered or reaching out to or following up with a contact. If you *work through* your lack of motivation on the days when you have none, you'll actually feel better for having taken action, and it will build your stamina to keep going. Take pride in building a reliable work ethic—it's an important and valuable asset. It will help carry you through the rough spots and it will stand you in good stead when you do land a job. It will make you a more valuable employee.

Feeling unconfident? Go back to your list of strengths from Chapter 1 and affirm the success you have in other parts of your life. Use this as a foundation to keep building. If you build a process, little by little you will feel more confident that it will get you where you need to go.

Reach out to a trusted friend or mentor for a pep talk. They can help! Often, they've been through it themselves.

When all else fails, say to yourself, "Ass in chair," then do it and get to work, even if you are not feeling it.

Still feeling stuck? Look for simple things you can do without too much thought, like researching contacts. It may help you "warm up" and move into tougher tasks. Even when it doesn't, you'll have the satisfaction of knowing you kept moving forward and got something done, despite feeling down. It will help make it easier to get started tomorrow.

Build Your Strategy: Envision Target Employment Opportunities

As you think about the job you want, refine your search to include companies, sectors, and locations that are reasonable, even if not ideal. As you begin to identify companies in your target, think about *the entire target*, not *just* the bull's-eye, which significantly limits your options. Don't focus too much on the "perfect" while ignoring the "good," since the "good" can be a stepping stone to the "better." Besides, the "good" will help you pay your bills, reduce your anxiety and build your self-esteem.

Likewise, you want to think of the target as a defined field of jobs that will help you focus on your search. It is generally counterproductive to think, "I'm open to anything!" This leaves you without a clear direction and can scatter your energies. It's time to find a reasonable range of options to consider.

For example, you may start out thinking,

"My dream job is working as a copywriter in advertising."

That's a fine goal, but the field is extremely competitive and you may not have a competitive portfolio and credentials at this time. But you may genuinely have a talent and interest to work in advertising.

Time to expand your thinking to something like: *"I'm excited about a career in advertising as a creative, but I'm also a good strategic thinker, have great teamwork and organization skills, and I'm excited about finding ways to connect clients with target audiences."*

This opens you up to apply for other posts in advertising that can lead to an equally rewarding career in management, planning or media buying, or could be a way for you to transition into more creative roles, possibly including copywriting, depending on your strengths.

Taking a step further, even as you are targeting a broader type of job, try to remain open to opportunities that may come your way, which speak to your interests and strengths and which you may not have considered.

Start With Research

Begin by doing your homework on available job openings and by identifying possible companies that may not have job openings listed currently but which may be a good fit.

- Stay current with job titles and descriptions that relate to your field. Some jobs will use different titles for similar roles. For example, an agency account coordinator job probably performs similar tasks to an assistant account executive. Working in-house at a company, the job title might be assistant manager. All are entry-level titles that might be appropriate if you are just starting out.
- Note the skills you have that sync with the job descriptions. This will be important for your resume and cover letters.
- Also note the skills you may *lack* for a job. Does that telegraph any weaknesses you may have that you need to shore up? If so, try to address this now. (See Chapter 1.)
- If you don't meet key criteria, like required years of experience, should you even be applying for this job? Probably not.
- Be aware of possible job titles and descriptions that fit your expertise and direction.
- Go to Indeed.com and do a key word search for your preferred area.
- Google job titles and descriptions that you are aiming for.

Plan to start with 30 companies. Rank them by:

- Obvious picks (preference and strong fit).
- Less obvious: Look outside the bull's-eye, but still within the target area.

Proactively pick industries based on their focus, such as sports, environmental, political, consumer, technology, health care, beauty, and so on, You can also choose businesses that you personally admire because of their social ethic.

Use LinkedIn, Google, Indeed, Glassdoor, or other platforms where companies on your target list may have a presence to better understand their needs, as it relates to your expertise and interest.

Think about *the employers'* needs around digital marketing, social media, advertising, public relations or other related areas where you have the know-how and interest to make a contribution.

Build a Network List (Then Keep Adding!)

Companies generally fill jobs in one of four ways:

- Internal hires
- Recruiter referrals
- Online advertised posts
- Networking

While the first three are good job funnels, networking through industry, friends, and acquaintances is by far the most valuable way to find a job. Hubspot[1] reports that in a 2020 survey on LinkedIn, the majority of respondents said they were hired as a result of someone they knew making an introduction or a connection.

Building a strong network is probably the most important and effective way to invest in your job hunt. (See Chapter 4.)

Start by making a list in the form of a table of the professionals you currently know who can serve as possible leads. They themselves may not have a direct company contact, but they may know people who are connected to a job you seek. Even if they don't know someone now, they can act as part of your "antenna" for relevant contacts and even job leads that may come their way in the future. Include their name, how you know them, e-mail, telephone, or other contact info and date of your most recent contact.

People in your network may include:

- Your current or former professors (especially in related disciplines).

- Alumni and friends from your college now working in a related industry.
- Other professionals you have met through your job (get business cards).
- Church or community groups, or even people you meet on your job or in daily life.
- Professional organization members such as those in PRSSA or AAF.

Your Personal Brand Brief

A job search plan is your one-page road map that highlights your core professional strengths and the kind of jobs you're seeking. This is NOT a resume, but essentially helps someone in your network easily grasp your thinking regarding your professional goals.

Your Positioning Statement: Who you are today.

This is a brief statement that succinctly states your core professional strengths as of now, and defines the target post you are seeking.

Example: "I'm a high achieving college graduate (degree in XX), with experience in YY, seeking an entry-level position in ZZ that builds on my academic training and workplace experience, along with my club leadership roles."

List your core competencies: You already did this work in Chapter 1, so feel free to upload the professional competencies you included (and some of the new ones that you are developing, having addressed them in your "weaknesses" section). These should support your positioning statement as evidence that you are qualified for the job you are seeking, even without direct experience.

List the target companies/agencies/organizations where you are seeking a position. Be sure to research and note the company location, size, and specialty. If helpful, you can create separate columns for agencies, companies, and organizations, and you can also differentiate them by size or specialty, for example, not-for-profit sector versus private sector, or health care versus consumer.

Perspectives: Isabella Santana, Manager, Integrated Media Planning, OMD

I started my job hunt five months before graduation. Despite taking six varied internships, I had difficulty deciding what career direction to pursue. I had experience in design branding and pop-up event planning for start-up clients, digital content creation and analytics, and social media community management for a nonprofit organization. But none of them gave me a clear career direction that I was excited about.

To add focus, one of my mentors suggested doing a self-assessment of my skills and work style by listing what I liked and disliked about each internship. This affirmed that I love research, I'm good at project management, and I'm curious about what's behind a strategic decision.

My mentor also networked me to professionals to learn if I might be a good fit for their areas of expertise. These interviews made me more comfortable talking to people with different communication styles and making better connections with each person.

I tracked each contact and job application on a Google sheet, including who I contacted, when I made contact, what were the next steps, and what happened.

It all came together at a job fair hosted by CCNY's Ad/PR program. When I met the recruiter for a media agency, everything clicked. I saw that media planning was a career that played to my strengths and interests.

Make Your Network Work for You

Your next step is to build a relationship with each individual in your network so that they understand where you are in your job search and what your goals are. Once you identify those in your initial network, reach out to each person personally via e-mail to request a meeting, in person, online or by phone. This will "activate" your network so that when someone in the network hears of someone or something relevant, they will be more likely to think of and contact you.

Do not ask if they know of a job opening, if they have any contact to get you a job, or if they can hire you! In almost all cases the answers to these questions will be "No," which likely ends the conversation before it even begins. Instead, try the following:

- Tell them that you are embarking on your job hunt and are gathering information.
- Ask what *they* are doing and what *they* are hearing about in a related industry.
- Ask if you can share your job search plan for their feedback.
- Ask if you can stay in touch with them either monthly or bimonthly.
- Ask if they can refer you to other people who would be worthwhile for you to talk to, even if there's no specific job opening. This is *crucial* because it builds your network (your antenna) and ultimately moves you closer to where you need to go.
- Email a thank you note *within 24 hours* expressing your gratitude for their help and informing them when you will follow up.

Sharing Your Document

Once your planning document is finalized, it's time to share it with your network. You can opt to share it with a select group of professionals with whom you have the strongest relationships, or you can expand your shares, depending on your relationship with each person.

Send a personalized e-mail to each selected professional with your document attached. Ask them to review your document with their feedback, or request a 15-minute phone session to discuss your document and get their feedback. (Time permitting, the phone session may be easier for your contact, since it minimizes the contact's efforts.)

Once they have had time to review your document, questions to ask are as follows:

- Do you think this list of target companies is appropriate for my experience?
- Are there any companies I should add or delete?
- Do you know anyone at any of the companies on this list?
- Would you be willing to make an introduction to your contact for an exploratory interview?

Use Feedback Constructively

The feedback you receive should help you to keep refining your document and focus on the kinds of organizations and jobs of most interest to you and that suit your strengths. Use this feedback to update your work plan, and to keep the engagement going with your network.

To track your progress, create a computer file, spreadsheet, or other list of your contact dates and feedback.

Remember to always email a thank you note to any person in your network who provides input, support, or guidance throughout, and try to keep them updated periodically on your progress. Do not take your network for granted.

Chapter Wrap Up

- You have identified possible jobs that suit your skills and interests and have expanded your thinking beyond a narrow target.
- You have identified other professionals or people in your circle who could provide valuable feedback and networking.
- You have created a plan as a foundation for your job search.

Now it's time to craft your resume and cover letter. Get ready for prime time!

CHAPTER 6

Your Brand Essentials = Resume + Cover Letter + Social Media

Be yourself, but always your better self.

—Karl G. Maeser

Everything you post on social media and send to recruiting professionals makes up your professional brand, so it needs to be perfect. If your copy shows you are strategic and is professionally presented (clean, neat, no grammatical/mechanical errors), you'll have a greater chance of being competitive for a job. Likewise, sloppily written copy and/or content that does not clearly address the interests of those you are targeting is likely to be ignored or rejected. It's important to craft your documents and social media posts very carefully before you share them publicly to ensure that you are presenting yourself in the best possible light.

This chapter addresses ways to help you maximize the effectiveness of your documents. We'll start with your social media, since this platform has 24/7 access to recruiters. Then we'll look at how best to craft your resume and cover letters for more targeted outreach.

Your Social Media: Job Magnet, Turn-off, or Black Hole?

A professional social media presence is essential for your job hunt and could bolster your chance for being hired—or tank it. Simply put, if *you* do not pay close attention to how you present yourself in a way that shows mature and professional judgment, how can an employer or client trust you to be prudent and professional in what you say about them (or anything else) on a public platform?

For starters, it's a good idea to do a Google search of your name every so often to see what comes up. If there are links to social media sites (Instagram, X-formally known as Twitter, TikTok, Facebook) that include images or content that would embarrass you to have employers see (or might embarrass your employers), you would be wise to delete the images or content immediately. Remember, you are now presenting your professional brand, so that requires a different "sniff test" for what is appropriate to share publicly, or not.

If you feel strongly about keeping questionable content, make sure your social media settings ensure that the content can be accessed only by those you want to do so and that it cannot be found in a general search. But remember that these social media settings may not be totally reliable in restricting access, especially if your professional connections also become social media connections.

I have worked with students who were competitive for certain jobs, but once the prospective employers did a search of the students' social media and found offensive or inappropriate comments or feeds, the employers dropped the candidates like a hot potato. Be aware that others will do a social media search on your name, so it's better to know how you may be perceived and to address it before your go full throttle with your job search.

Because this is a digital world, having a professional digital presence is a must, even if you are only on LinkedIn. Having zero digital presence could be construed as an indication that you are not savvy about social media and how relationships are built, plus it makes it harder for professionals to find you.

LinkedIn

While your resume and cover letter are your core tools to reach out proactively for job opportunities in your target field, your social media presence, especially LinkedIn, is key to having businesses locate you as a prospective employee, and once they do, to affirm your professionalism and brand.

There are a few essential elements to creating a strong LinkedIn profile :

Create a professional headline that showcases your expertise.
Focus on what you have to offer to communications hiring professionals (or other fields that interest you), and incorporate keywords to maximize search engine optimization (SEO) that people will use to find you. For example, if you are going for a public relations post, you may want to use such keywords as "media relations/influencer expertise, social media marketing, writing/storytelling" or others that are essential aspects of the job you seek.

Create a strong summary that showcases your passion for your profession. Include additional details about related internships, projects, or other related experiences that speak to your professionalism. Remember to "show, don't tell," by including content that highlights relevant and up-to-date experience and that also helps you stand out as an individual who is more than just your skills. This can show your success and tenacity in other areas where you have succeeded against adversity, as well as your commitment and passion for excellence.

One note of caution: don't narrow your description so much as to hurt your chances of being considered for posts that may be out of your bull's-eye but could still be good options for you. Keep your content focused, but not too limited in scope. You may dream of going into fashion PR, but don't be so explicit as to hurt your chances of attracting interest by HR professionals in related fields, such as beauty.

Include a photo that shows you at your professional best. While you don't have to hire a professional photographer, you want an

---

*Here are two useful online resources on creating a better LinkedIn profile:
(1) www.linkedin.com/business/sales/blog/profile-best-practices/17-steps-to-a
-better-linkedin-profile-in-2017
(2) https://nealschaffer.com/linkedin-best-practices/

image that is crisp and clear, with good lighting. Your image should fill the frame (preferably a head and shoulders shot) and should not include extraneous props or distractions from showing off your professionalism. An upbeat facial expression is preferable to one that is too solemn. Try to showcase a positive and professional side of you that someone would want to interact with at a job. Dress should be conservative and professional, similar to what you might wear for an interview (see Chapter 7). Do not let what you wear, or the accessories you choose, overpower you, or diminish your professionalism.

Highlight your skills that are relevant to the job you are seeking. If possible, ask other professionals who know your work to endorse those skills by inviting them to comment on your site. The "Recommendations" section of your LinkedIn profile is one good place to do this. When appropriate you can return the favor on their profiles.

Showcase your value by sharing related content. Sharing or commenting on current trade industry news about marketing communications, white papers on trends, or other content that relates to the field you hope to enter is an important way to show your passion and proactivity in staying current. This will help prospective employers see you as someone who adds value and is highly engaged, a huge plus. If you have more to say on a current topic, posting a brief but relevant article on LinkedIn can be another good way to showcase your knowledge.

Use your LinkedIn profile as a networking tool. If there's a particular person you would like to reach out to and someone you know is connected to them on LinkedIn, you can ask your connection to introduce you by forwarding your profile electronically, right on the LinkedIn platform, with a cover note to the person in question. If that person is open to it, you may then be able to set up a direct networking call. This is a powerful way to broaden your network and even make inside connections with businesses your admire and aspire to work for.

Your Online Portfolio

Another important online tool is creating a website with a portfolio of professional work, especially important if you are pursuing a job in the advertising industry or as a strategist. You'll want to make it easy for a prospective employer to see samples of your related work, especially if they are strong. Make sure that you not only show the output, but that you also include some of the strategic thinking behind it to showcase how you effectively solved a client's problem.

Note: If the work was done for a prior employer, make sure that it is "shareable" and does not reflect any proprietary information.

Your online portfolio is part of your brand too, so use simple and consistent fonts/colors that unify and connect all aspects of your online presence. You can find templates for portfolios that suit your work online, such as on Canva.

You can link this to your LinkedIn profile to make it easy for professionals to see.

Make sure to include your LinkedIn and online portfolio links on your resume, as well.

Your Business Card

Business cards are a powerful part of your professional brand and arsenal, even as a student. Do not assume that LinkedIn is a substitute for a business card. They serve different functions and work together to extend your reach. So, you need both! Always keep a few business cards in your wallet, since you never know whom you'll meet or when.

Business cards are an important personal branding tool at all professional levels and have the power to enhance opportunities well beyond an initial meeting. Once you secure your first job, it's likely that your employer will give you business cards that are branded with company information. For now, you don't need to be employed to have one. Before you actively begin applying to internships and jobs, and prior to active networking at events, order your own business cards. You can get about 100 cards for a few dollars from online sites, which you can Google.

Do not be overly concerned about a fancy design or graphics. Best to keep the font simple, professional, and easy to read. (White print on a black background is not easy to read, for example, even if you think it looks cool and helps you stand out).

Your card should include the following:

- **Side One:**
    - o Your name (as it appears on your LinkedIn page and resume)
    - o Current status: For example, Marketing Communications major. Make sure your status is listed the same way it appears on your LinkedIn so that people can easily find you, especially if there is more than one person on LinkedIn with your same first and last names.
    - o Other leadership/professional titles, if relevant, such as President, PRSSA, or AAF chapter (include college name)
    - o LinkedIn address
    - o Cell phone
    - o Email address
- **Side Two (optional, and can increase printing costs):**
    - o Highlights of your qualifications: professional skills and experience that define your core strengths.

Resume and Cover Letter = Your Brand Ambassadors

Your resume and cover letter are generally the first interactions a prospective employer will have with you. Think of them as your brand "ambassadors," paving the way for future contact, an interview and hopefully, a job offer. That means the content (what you say) and presentation (how you say it) need to be substantive, targeted, and perfect.

Employers get hundreds of applications, so work carefully and diligently to present yourself in the best light. In fact, employers use sloppily written cover letters or resumes as a reason to *weed out* candidates, even when their credentials are good. If you are sloppy in how you present yourself when you have total control over your information, you are also likely to be sloppy in your professional work. Not a desirable trait.

As a result, take extra time to ensure that everything you write is professional in tone, grammar, and layout, and is targeted to the job for which you are applying.

Think Strategically

Many people draft their resume and cover letter in a vacuum, keeping in mind only *their* professional goals and experience. While these documents represent you, that's not all you need to consider.

Before you draft your documents, first consider *who* will read these documents and what *their needs* are. Remember, a recruiter, talent acquisition, account professional, or even an AI "spider" bot, will be evaluating your application materials based on the job description. Having a clear understanding of what a potential employer values in experience and skills will help you create a more targeted and effective document. The key is looking carefully at the job description and highlighting in your resume and cover letter as many of the listed competencies as you possess.

Generally, a "one size fits all" resume and cover letter are not sufficient to speak to the needs of every job you apply for. Think about having tweaked versions that address *each* job description (or at least each category of job you're interested in). Be sure to label your documents carefully (in the filenames if possible) so you don't upload the wrong cover letter and resume! Easy to do, embarrassing to fix, and your carelessness in uploading the wrong cover letter or resume could be a deal-breaker.

As you craft your documents, communicate clearly and succinctly what you offer an employer, regardless of whether you think this is your "dream job." While your "dream job" may be important to you, it's not the most important criterion for the employer. Remember, they are looking at your information in terms of *what you can do for them*, not what they can do for you!

Be Persuasive: Connect the Dots

Think of your resume and cover letter as a polished showcase of your experience to build a persuasive case to get hired. It is not effective to simply include information on a page and hope it will connect with the reader. Remember you are applying as a professional communicator and your own materials are evidence of your communications abilities.

Your resume and cover letter need to *speak to the prospective employer's needs*. If you're replying to a job posting, read it thoroughly and note all the areas where you meet the required skills/experience. You may not meet them all, but that's okay. If you meet most of the core requirements, apply.

Your task is to highlight your skills and related experience that the employer wants, so take time to make it easy for the employer to see that you are a strong candidate, based on the job description.

Exercise

Here's a generic internship description to practice highlighting your relevant skills.

If you were applying for this job, list the keywords, qualities, and skills in the job description that you would highlight to show your competitiveness for this opportunity. ***Hint:*** *Look at the specific skills that are mentioned that you have and for which you can show examples; how your interests/experience coincides with the industry; and other classroom or workplace experience that speaks to the specifics listed. Remember, you don't have to show that you are a match for everything, just a few important areas.*

XYZ Agency seeks public relations intern with consumer group. 40 hours/week, $20/hr.

Seeking PR intern who is passionate about public relations for consumer brands. Strategic thinker who shows creativity and ability to share brand's news in press and on social media platforms in compelling ways that connect with target audiences. Successful candidate will demonstrate strong oral and written professional communication skills.

Candidate is detail-oriented and is adept at working effectively on teams or independently in fast-paced environment. Skilled in MS

Outlook, Excel, and PowerPoint. Knowledge of Cision and media monitoring programs a plus.

As an intern, you will conduct research, brainstorm campaign ideas, craft tactical media materials, pitch stories to media, monitor traditional and social coverage, and participate in event logistics planning and execution.

Qualified candidate is a college senior or recent graduate, a go-getter who has completed at least one public relations internship or has relevant experience that demonstrates competencies.

Your Resume

As you craft your resume, it's a good idea to research entry-level job descriptions in the field you want to enter to get a sense of the skills and industry jargon that are valued. Where appropriate, build this language into your actual resume, another indicator that you are up to speed on industry skill sets and terminology.

If you see industry terminology, acronyms, or skills in the job descriptions you find, which you are not familiar with, be sure to Google them so you will know what they mean.

Write the resume content before thinking about the finished layout. Try to keep your resume to *one page*. (In the future, when you have more experience, two pages may be appropriate, but not when you are an entry-level candidate.) You'll need to be targeted and selective with the information you include, which may mean leaving out some less relevant experience from college or even early work experience.

Content

There are many useful resume approaches, but I find that the following format and content areas are effective ways to showcase your skills, especially when entering the job market in a new area. The resume format you use now will likely evolve and change over time, just as your career will evolve. Resumes (and careers) are works in progress as you grow, so be prepared to revise as you progress.

Name/Contact Info

Your resume heading includes your name, e-mail, LinkedIn address, and phone. Your name should be prominent (bold, at least 16-point type), but should not take up huge space on the page. The rest of the information can be smaller but still legible type.

Core Qualifications

A short statement highlighting the **relevant** experience and training you have for the job to which you're applying. It can be three or four lines long. Lead with your strongest professional strengths.

For example:

> Recent college graduate with in-depth training in Digital Marketing/SEO/Facebook Ads. Internship/workplace experience in web design and retail sales. Strong oral/written communications and research skills. Seeking entry-level post in digital marketing.

You can also start with a descriptive phrase:

> Results-driven communications major with agency internship experience in XYZ.
>
> or
>
> High-achieving college graduate with in-depth training in data analytics and professional experience in XYZ.

Skills

This can be a subset of your core qualifications. Break skills into clear categories that are most relevant to your job. Think about the priorities of the employers, then list them in that order:

- *Computer skills*: Microsoft Office (Excel proficient), Adobe, InDesign, Tableau.

- *Digital platforms:* Google Analytics, Cision, Hootsuite, (list others as appropriate, but do *not* use the word "etc.").
- *Languages:* (only if multilingual) indicate oral and written proficiency.

To List or Not to List: Hard Skills/Soft Skills?

Listing the relevant hard skills is key. But, in general, including soft skills, such as being "detail-oriented, team-player, self-starter" will not add to your competitive edge. It's better to showcase these aspects of your professionalism through tangible examples under your job descriptions, rather than just including a laundry list of generic qualities. If you want to talk about soft skills, save it for your cover letter where you can briefly elaborate on those skills that helped you bring value to your employer.

Education

(*If your Experience is stronger, include this before Education. Otherwise, list your Education credentials after your Core Qualifications.*)

Your college name, city, state.

BA (BS) in Major, month/year of graduation (do not include years attended). You can include your GPA if 3.0 or higher (rounded to one digit after the decimal point) OR if you graduated with honors, include *Cum Laude, Magna Cum Laude, or Summa Cum Laude* (or other relevant honor, such as *with High Honors*) in italics.

Include minor, especially if relevant to the job or field.

(OPTIONAL) *Related Coursework:* Include the *most relevant and advanced* classes first (not essential, but it can help if relevant). Or, if you have taken additional workshops, such as Google Analytics or others, include them.

Put Associates Degree (if you have one) below with degree/year and college.

Do *not* include high school information, unless it is a specialized high school that ties into your professional training.

If you are still in college, you can list your credentials as: BA Candidate in Major: Expected month/year. Include your GPA if strong (above 3.0).

Experience

List your most relevant and recent job experience here. Include the name of the business and its location and your time of service. If you have done an internship in the field you are applying for, list that first under experience, even if you have held other more recent or longer-term jobs.

You can either list the company first and your job title under it, or put your job title first and the company beneath it.

Below each job title, use bullets to showcase your responsibilities and accomplishments. Consider what is most relevant to the job you are applying for. But also include jobs such as retail, customer service, child care, or others, since it shows that you have held jobs and have had responsibility, even if not directly related to this post.

Beneath your job listing, bullet the essential job functions. List the most important and relevant tasks first (and most basic or menial last). Lead with *active* verbs to show what you did, as in the following example. If you are still in the job, use present tense active verbs (e.g., *manage*). If it's a job from your past, use past tense (*managed*). Be consistent in each of your bullets.

Where possible, showcase the *RESULTS* of your work by quantifying the value you brought.

Here's an example:

Experience

- Name of Company, City, State Starting Month/Year to Ending Month/Year

---

- **Job title**
  - Managed…
  - Oversaw…
  - Created…
  - Coordinated…
  - Generated 50 percent increase in store sales over three months. (Quantify results).
  - Named outstanding employee X times for exceeding sales quotas.

If there is a gap in your employment, that's okay. Be prepared to address this briefly in your cover letter and in your interview. If you have enough other strong qualifications, employers will understand.

Clubs/Leadership

If you have experience as a member of a student professional club (such as PRSSA or AAF) you can include it under "Experience." If you have been a club leader or there is another reason to highlight your contributions, you can give it a separate section headed '*Clubs/Leadership*' after '*Experience*.'

Awards and Honors

If these are job related, include them with related job description (*see "Named outstanding employee…"* previously). If academic related, you can list them further down on your resume. List the honor and year received. If it's unclear what the award is for, then provide a brief description to help the reader understand its significance.

Community Service/Volunteerism

If you have contributed to your community or to a recognized charity or other good cause in a meaningful way, it is a nice addition to your resume because it shows you as a caring, proactive, and multidimensional person. List the most recent and relevant service you have provided, including the name of the organization, your role, and dates. If your contributions relate to the job you are applying for, indicate your role under the related job description, as you did your job. For example: *"Organized Employee Volunteer Day for Habitat for Humanity."*

Proofread, Proofread, and Proofread Again!

Make sure you proof your resume carefully for correct facts, spelling, grammar, capitalization, and consistent use of fonts and periods and other punctuation. Ideally, it's a good habit to do this every time you send it out. The same applies to e-mails and cover letters, since typos can be annoying and undermine your sales pitch. The habit will also keep helping you after you get the job.

Do not proof when you are tired or under deadline, as it will increase the likelihood of your being sloppy and missing errors. Leave yourself plenty of time to write the document, walk away from it, and then come back to it with fresh eyes. The more familiar you are with your document, the *harder* it will be to look critically at the printed page without skimming. Give yourself ample time to look at your document.

If possible, find another pair of trusted eyes to review your document. You can also go back to a mentor in your network and ask them to review your document. If you do this, always try to give them several days to get back to you. You never want to ask for a fast turn-around. It's unprofessional and discourteous. Asking for this kind of assistance has the added benefit of helping to strengthen your relationship with your mentor and helps them feel connected to you and stay updated on your progress, in case they hear of something or someone relevant to your search.

Layout

Your resume's design and readability are two important considerations beyond the content. If your resume is sloppily laid out on the page, or is hard to read, this does not represent you at your professional best. It can be another reason to be disqualified for a post early on. Take care of your layout, font, and color choices, if you are not just using black and white. Make sure your font size is large enough to be read easily, but not too large. Keep your page margins to at least one inch and align your left margins for a clean and neat layout.

On first reading, recruiters will generally skim resumes (or use software or AI) to look for keywords in your experience that speak to the qualifications they seek. Their eyes will generally follow a "Z" path on the page (upper left to upper right, then lower left to lower right). That's an essential reason to get keywords and information toward the top of the page under "Core Qualifications" and "Skills." You want to grab someone's interest on top of the page quickly to get them to read more closely.

The layout should support your content. Unless you are going for a graphic design job, *what you say is much more important than the graphics*. Make sure your layout and graphics are easy to read and look professional.

Thanks to Microsoft Word, it's easy to create a document with a clear layout, an easy-to-read font, and effective use of **bold,** *italics,* and • bullets. You can also look at any number of free online templates or at sites like Canva to select your best design. Don't go overboard with lots of fonts and colors. Keep your resume elegant, simple, and easy to read. Do not let a fancy font get in the way of clarity.

To prioritize what to include and where to put it, think of the page as "real estate" and consider how much space each section takes up on the page. For example, while your name should be prominent, having it take up a full inch or more, as some templates show, is likely unnecessary, especially if it squeezes you for space for something more important. It's better to dedicate as much of the page as possible to content relating to the skills and experience for the job you want. These are your real selling points.

Photo or No Photo?

While some resume formats build in a place for a photo, it's better not to include a photo. Better to have a professional photo of yourself on your LinkedIn page, and provide a link to that page in the top heading. If someone is interested, they'll go to LinkedIn, which they may be using to vet you anyway, and they'll see your photo there. Use your available page "real estate" to highlight substantive and relevant information about yourself. (Figure 6.1)

Cover Letter

While many jobs ask applicants to just post a resume, there may be occasions where employers also want to see a cover letter. Owing to the increased use of digital programs that help employers weed out candidates using key word searches for resumes, cover letters often don't get read. However, sometimes cover letters can be an important addition to your outreach and can help you get your "foot in the door" to secure an interview beyond just your resume.

A cover letter is NOT your resume in prose form. This is a separate document that complements and expands on the information in your resume, and speaks to the *specific* job and interests of the employer to whom you are writing. Think of it as a sales pitch letter that gives you another opportunity to showcase who you are and what makes you stand out. It's a succinctly written form of your elevator pitch.

Many employers also use cover letters to get a sense of your ability to communicate well in writing and to gauge your professionalism. So it's important to *tailor each cover letter to the job you are applying for.* It is ineffective to have a generic "Dear Hiring Manager" salutation and form letter that you submit to every job you are applying for. A generic letter does not speak to the employer's specific needs, nor does it show them that you took the time to really understand what *their* job is all about. *Failure to customize each of your letters to the specific job is a key reason you can be eliminated from consideration.*

That being said, there is core information that may be appropriate to include in every letter, as long as elements are customized to each job.

FIRST LAST

CONTACT

(555) 123-4567

FIRSTLAST@GMAIL.COM

HTTPS://WWW.LINKEDIN.COM/
IN/FIRSTLAST

PROFILE

Proactive public relations professional
driven by curiosity and positive
energy with internship, leadership,
event planning and research
experience.

SKILLS

- Canva
- Cision
- Meltwater
- Muck Rack
- Coverage Book
- Microsoft Office
- Social media
- Advanced Spanish

EDUCATION

**BA IN COMMUNICATIONS,
CONCENTRATION IN PUBLIC
RELATIONS AND ADVERTISING**
CITY COLLEGE OF NY | SPRING 2020
GPA: 4.0
Coursework: Advertising and Public
Relations Workshop, Public Relations
Writing, Advertising Management,
Advertising Planning, Corporate
Communications, Social Media
Strategies, Internet Marketing, Data
Mining and Analytics, Market Research,
Copywriting, Ethics, Microeconomics.

EXPERIENCE

MEDIA RELATIONS INTERN
ROONEYPARTNERS | JANUARY 2020 - MAY 2020, JUNE 2019 -
AUGUST 2019

- Contacted journalists by email and phone, edited press
  releases and pitches, built targeted media lists, coverage
  books, and briefing documents. Helped secure media
  placements in top-tier and trade publications.

PUBLIC RELATIONS INTERN
DERRIS | SEPTEMBER 2019 - DECEMBER 2019

- Worked on client-facing and internal materials for accounts
  like Warby Parker, Reformation, Homebound, Lola, and Harry's.

BUSINESS DEVELOPMENT RESEARCH ASSISTANT
THE ART STEVENS GROUP | JULY 2018 - OCTOBER 2019

- Performed research to find new clients for a firm specializing
  in mergers and acquisitions in the communications industry.
- Responsibilities included identifying agencies that met
  specific criteria, i.e., revenue, location, employee count, and
  capabilities. Monitored trade publications for relevant news.

PROFESSIONAL ORGANIZATION WORK

BIG APPLE AWARDS COMMITTEE MEMBER
PRSA-NY | JANUARY 2020 - CURRENT

- Increase income by recognizing and contacting interested
  parties for award entry submissions and sponsorships. Assist
  fellow committee members with event planning.

VICE PRESIDENT
PRSSA CITY COLLEGE CHAPTER | MAY 2019 - MAY 2020

- Communicated with faculty advisors, fellow club leaders, and
  members to plan meetings and events. Previously Event
  Coordinator for Spring 2019.

AWARDS AND ACCOMPLISHMENTS

**ART STEVENS PRSA-NY/CCNY SCHOLAR FOR EXCELLENCE IN
PUBLIC RELATIONS**
APRIL 2019

- Chosen in recognition of academic record, professional work,
  PRSSA involvement, and enthusiasm to join the PR industry.

SJ LEVY FELLOWSHIP FOR FUTURE LEADERS
FALL 2018 - SUMMER 2019

- Fellows receive education, training, and mentorship
  concerning business culture with an emphasis on ethics.

Figure 6.1 Resume

Your cover letter should be in a professional business letter format that explains why *you* are a good fit for this specific job. It is *not* about your passions, your life history, and definitely not about how much you want this job. Generally, include the following:

- A professional salutation to the addressee.
- An opening statement, including the *exact* title of the job you are applying for at the specific company.
- Your academic/work status now.
- Evidence of your qualifications for the job for which you're applying.
- An option to address any glaring deficits that you want to explain.
- Your experience at a specific job as it relates to the employer's specific needs, beyond what's already in your resume.
- Why you are interested in this particular job and business (do your homework on that business to find something genuine to share about why you want "this" job, not just "any" job).
- Information on how to reach you.
- Thank them for their consideration.

Just like your resume, your cover letter *must* have perfect grammar, spelling, and punctuation. You also need to proofread carefully and be certain you are uploading the proper letter to its designated recipient.

Sample Cover Letter Format

- **E-mail subject line:** Your Name: Applicant for [NAME OF POST]
- **Salutation:** (*your greeting matters*)
   o If you don't know who is reading your document, you can say "Dear Hiring Manager."
   o Always use a name, if you have one. Dear Mr. Smith, or Dear Ms. Sanchez, Dear Mx. Jones.
   o Do not use Mrs. or Miss.
   o Do not address them by just their first name if you do not know them personally.
   o If you don't know the person's gender, use first and second names: Dear Francis Jones.

The Body

Cover letters should be kept to one page, ideally to three or four succinct paragraphs, single spaced. Double space between paragraphs. You want your letter to be easy to read. Do not write large blocks of type that make it hard to read. Expect people to skim your letter.

As with all good writing, start each paragraph with a strong topic sentence to lead the reader.

Sample Copy

First Paragraph

I'm writing to apply for a position as a digital marketing associate with XYZ Company. As a recent college graduate with specialized training in SEO/SEM, I have the skills and experience that will allow me to bring value to your team.

Second Paragraph

This provides an overview showing that you have either related experience or coursework/training to meet the needs of the employer. You should highlight your most important professional experience and soft skills (e.g., team player, quick study, multitasker, meets deadlines, strong communicator).

I come to NAME OF ORGANIZATION with experience in WHAT? [*List key organizations where you worked and how you brought professional or relevant value.*]

OR

I come to NAME OF ORGANIZATION with a strong foundation through a degree in communications (or the COOP Careers program). [*Then go into detail about what you learned, as it applies to the job.*]

OR

I have additional work experience in retail sales working for ABC. In this capacity I DID WHAT? [*Here is a chance to discuss your additional qualifications and professionalism (Organization, adaptability, met deadlines, set priorities, and took pride in delivering excellent work).*]

Third Paragraph

Tells why you want to work for THEM and affirm how you'll contribute (even *if it's not your favorite opportunity*).

I'm especially excited about this position because of WHY SPECIFICALLY THEM? Or, if not your primary job choice, you can say, I'm excited about helping clients and the company to succeed. [*Show you did your research. This is **not** about what they can do for you. **It's about what you can do for them.***]

Fourth Paragraph

Close out the letter graciously, show you are open to follow up.

Thank you in advance for your consideration. I would welcome the chance to meet with you or to talk by phone at your earliest convenience. You can reach me at (xxx) xxx-xxxx or e-mail@e-mail.com.

Sincerely,
Your name

Sample Cover Letter Template

Dear Hiring Manager:

I am writing to apply for the digital account coordinator position at NAME OF COMPANY. (***NOTE:*** *If you were referred by someone say, I'm writing to apply for XYZ job at the recommendation of NAME OF PERSON.*)

I recently completed the COOP Careers Program in New York where I acquired essential skills in digital marketing, specifically in SEO/SEM and Facebook Ads. These skills, coupled with my undergraduate education and workplace experience, will enable me to be a strong contributor to your team.

OR YOU CAN SAY:

As a 2024 college graduate majoring in Communications, I acquired essential skills in public relations/advertising for an entry-level position in this field. As my resume indicates, I have prior work experience as a JOB TITLE for COMPANY. In this capacity, I brought my strong work ethic and professionalism to my employer. (*Or say something that demonstrates your relevant professionalism.*) In addition to my abilities and passion for digital marketing, I am hard working and have experience delivering excellent work under deadline. (*Or, add more personal qualities here that speak to your professionalism.*)

I am especially interested in this job because of NAME OF COMPANY'S QUALITY (*say something about the company that brands them based on their website copy or what you like about them*). (Try to make this authentic and not just copy lifted from their website. Show that you did your homework.)

I would welcome the opportunity to discuss this further. Please contact me via (your e-mail) or (your phone number). Thank you in advance for your time and consideration.

Sincerely,

Your first and last names

Phone

E-mail

Sample Cover Letter

Here is a sample cover letter sent via e-mail. Note: Your resume should be embedded in the e-mail body below your letter. Many businesses do not like opening attachments as it exposes them to computer viruses.

To: Hiringmanager@ABCAgency.com

Subject: Applicant for Associate's position: ABC Agency

Dear Hiring Manager,

I am writing to apply for the position of Associate at ABC Agency. After meeting with Jane Doe from your agency at CCNY's Career Fair and learning about the opportunities that you offer recent graduates, I was instantly intrigued. Given my studies in communications, my leadership role in my college's PRSSA chapter, two internships with public relations agencies, and my research experience for a public relations mergers and acquisitions firm, I know this would be a wonderful opportunity where I could bring value quickly.

As my resume below shows, I am majoring in Public Relations and Advertising at CCNY (graduating May, this year). Beyond my strong academic performance (GPA 4.0), I am vice president of my college's PRSSA chapter where I bring my leadership and vision to shape chapter programs. At my current internship at XYZ Agency, I've learned how to think strategically and successfully working on multiple account teams to address priorities and meet tight deadlines. During my media relations internship at HIJ Agency, I effectively engaged with journalists and improved at writing press materials. As a researcher for the Jane Doe Group, I have stayed abreast of the ways that public relations is constantly evolving. Supervisors praise me for my multitasking abilities to deliver professional work and my eagerness to learn and contribute to my team.

The opportunity to work for ABC Agency is especially appealing. I am interested in learning more about the financial, start-ups, and food, beverage, and nutrition sectors of public relations, an important part of your client roster. I am also attracted to your commitment to support new talent by matching your Associates' interests with an appropriate sector to help them learn and grow. I look forward to discussing this opportunity with you at your earliest convenience. Thank you in advance for your consideration.

Sincerely,

First Last

(555) 123-4567

firstlast@gmail.com

ChatGPT as an Aid

There is increasing discussion about using ChatGPT for cover letters (as well as many other applications). While it may be helpful to ask an AI to draft your cover letter, do NOT use this draft as your final letter. HR professionals are increasingly skilled at determining letters that were AI generated because they often have a generic and bland quality.

If you choose to use AI to help you with your cover letter, make sure you ask it to tailor each cover letter to the specific job you are applying for. Do not use a generic AI letter for all your job applications. It's not substantive and does not address the specific needs of the employer. Your letter will be more compelling if you include specifics about your work history and value and say why you are excited about *a particular job* opportunity in your own words.

While you should not rely on ChatGPT to write your letter, ChatGPT can help you to craft a stronger draft if you run your letter through the program and ask it to give you specific ways to strengthen your lead, reframe your strengths to target specific job demands, or to eliminate extraneous points.

Chapter Wrap Up

- You have started to think about your professional skills and experience in relation to the needs of the employers you hope will hire you.
- You have done a Google search of your name and are aware of any possible content that you may want to delete.
- You have created a strong LinkedIn profile that can help recruiters find you as a great match for their search.
- You have printed your own business cards for in-person networking.
- Your resume incorporates keywords and highlighted competencies from the job posting toward the top that makes it easy for a recruiter to see that you are a good match for their search.

- You have crafted a succinct cover letter for *each* job that builds on your resume to amplify your relevant skills and that speaks to the *specific* needs of the job you are applying for.
- You have proofread all your documents carefully.
- You have saved and labeled them under professional filenames that allow you to easily identify which version of your resume and cover letter corresponds to each type of job you apply for.

Time to get charged up for interviewing!

CHAPTER 7

The Application Cycle

Apply, Wait, Apply, Wait, Interview, Wait, Repeat Multiple Times

Success is not final; failure is not fatal: It is the courage to continue that counts.

—Winston S. Churchill

Once you have finessed your resume and cover letter, you are ready to play the application game. It can be a long process, so gear up for a marathon! Plan on applying to at least 30 positions generated from your strategic plan, job search, and network. Remember, some jobs will feel like they are a better fit than others. Stay focused on your area of expertise and experience, but don't narrow your focus so much as to exclude jobs that may still be a reasonably good fit. A decent job that you get is way better than the perfect job that you never find.

What to Expect Once You Apply

Job hunting etiquette has vastly changed in today's landscape. This is due in part to recruiter job demands and in part to the high volume of applications that come through digital platforms, as well as to generational changes.

Unfortunately, because of the huge number of applications many companies receive, you should expect to *not* hear back from a recruiter if they have eliminated you as a candidate for a job. You may not even get any confirmation that your application has been received. Recruiters and employers can ghost you, too. Sometimes your application will just seem to disappear into a black hole.

Feeling as though your applications are being sucked into a void is part of the process. To counteract the anxiety of waiting to hear back, once you apply to a job (even one your heart is set on) *immediately* move on to the next job application or networking call. It will help you avoid wasting time (and making yourself feel bad) hoping you land a gig, while being unproductive. Continuing to apply for other posts and generating additional leads until you have a job in hand also keeps you focused on other opportunities and invested in your goal. The networking, application, and interviewing process is your friend and will ultimately help you to succeed.

The same is true even if you get a job interview, because an interview does *not* mean you are sure to get the job. Companies and recruiters usually want to consider at least two or three candidates, which means there is almost always competition. Keep applying for other posts and try not to be too invested until you have a firm offer. (*Easier said than done.*)

How to Approach an Interview

Getting an interview is *not* a job offer, a mistake that many people make. The thinking is, "If I got to the interview stage, this is just a formality!" *It's not.* It's an opportunity to further showcase your professionalism and your personal qualities beyond your cover letter and resume. Chances are there will be several top candidates, possibly including internal candidates, who are invited to interview. Be prepared to present your best professional self by doing your homework on the company and the job for which you are interviewing.

Throughout the interview, you are pitching yourself as the employer's best choice. All your answers need to relate to *their* priorities and needs, based on the job description and what you have learned about the company.

One of the most important intangible traits a recruiter looks for is whether you are a "good fit" for their office/corporate culture and for a specific team of people. The traditional notion of "fit" looks at how well suited you are to a particular job and to the values and mission of a company and the company culture. This might include how effectively you work with the other members of your group to be a strong contributor and how well you would blend with the team's personalities and work styles to create greater efficiency and success.

Some hiring professionals prefer not to use the term "fit," because it assumes that there is a rigid set of criteria that candidates need to meet. Companies look for employees who could contribute to the business's mission and values by bringing their own perspectives and experiences to support and enhance company goals. They are assessing whether an employee will be productive and has character traits that will allow them to add value to their team, be collegial, and contribute to the overall success of the business.

On a broader level, recruiters also want to know that you are a match with the company culture. That means sharing their values, core beliefs, attitudes, and behaviors to help the company achieve its mission.

In a workplace world where diversity is increasingly valued, "fit" does not mean that you must look and think like everyone else. In fact, diversity of thought is highly sought after by many businesses (though not all). While you bring your own essential values and attitudes to any workplace, you will need to think honestly about whether you would be happy and comfortable working in a particular corporate culture and for clients whose values you can respect and embrace.

Here are some criteria that a recruiter will be thinking about:

- Do you have the skills and experience they need?
- Are you professional? (Have work experience that showcases your professionalism?)
- Do they feel comfortable around you?
- Do you feel comfortable around them?
- Have you done your homework on the company?
- Do you respect the company's mission and/or the clients for whom you'd be working?
- Do you present yourself as positive and energetic?
- Can you *hit the ground running*, dig in, learn and deliver?
- Can you demonstrate why you really want *this* job? (Not just *any* job.)

- Is there something they missed in your resume that makes you stand out (in either a good way or a not-so-good way)?

A Two-Way Street

While interviewers are assessing if you are a good fit for them, this is also your opportunity to determine if they are a good fit for you.

Here are some criteria for *you* to determine if you would want to work there. Your own observations are often a strong gauge of the "vibe" of the workplace, whether it's laid back, energized, frenzied, pressured, or hostile. But here are some other things to think about:

- Do I respect the kind of industry the company represents, or, if it's an agency, do I respect its clients?
- Do I feel respected and welcomed by the interviewer(s)?
- Does the interviewing team leave time for my questions?
- Do people seem happy to work there?
- Do you get a sense there is a welcoming and inclusive environment? Can I imagine myself going to work there?
- Am I excited about the actual job description?
- Does the job and team feel like a good fit for my skills?
- Will I be learning and supported?

Preparing for the Interview

Researching a company, and the interviewer, if possible, prior to your interview is essential for you to present your best self. It's also another opportunity to figure out if you would like to work there.

The basics of researching any company include the following:

- Look at the company's website to familiarize yourself with its mission and clients.
- Note significant news stories, case studies, and how they talk about client services.
- Carefully look at the language they use to differentiate themselves.

- Familiarize yourself with their social media engagement on LinkedIn, TikTok, Instagram, and X (formerly known as Twitter) or other relevant platforms.
- Google search their name to see what comes up and whether there are any red flags or things that you want to note and ask about or possibly mention as a positive in your interview.
- Look at their employee ratings on Glassdoor.com or other similar sites.
- If you know who your interviewer is, look at their LinkedIn profile and note important details or common interests that might be appropriate to mention in your interview. For example, if you both played the same sport or like the same hobby, that may be worth mentioning after you have established your credentials.

Interview Time: Keep Your Professional Game On!

Everyone gets nervous at interviews, but HR professionals are trained to put you at ease to help you deliver your best interview. While this can be effective in helping you relax, always keep your professional game on. Do not let down to reveal anything unprofessional. Interviewers are *not* your friends. They want to see how you maintain your professional energy and demeanor throughout! Imagine a microphone (or a video camera) being on. Do not say anything you might regret later—most likely you can't take it back.

You may feel you have great rapport that is genuine, but remember they are trying to create a connection with *everyone* they talk to. It's their job to make you *want* to work there. They will be showcasing the best parts of the job even while they are assessing your professionalism. Likewise, if you find yourself in an interview where the team makes you uncomfortable, that could be a red flag that it may not be a great fit for you.

Your goal is showcasing yourself as a positive, collaborative person who is easy to work with, delivers value, and enhances the team dynamics.

Dress for Success

Whether you are interviewing in person, on Zoom, or even with a bot on a screen, your professional image matters. This means you want to wear professional clothing that fits the workplace culture. Better to be slightly overdressed than underdressed, even in cultures where jeans and sneakers are the norm. On the flip side, you do not need to wear expensive designer clothing for most jobs. Whatever you choose, make sure your attire is neat, clean, and professional. Keep your hygiene professional too. Do not wear strong perfume or cologne. Make sure your breath is fresh.

- **For Women:** Blouse/blazer, slacks or skirt, low heels or flats are always appropriate. Low cut clothing is not appropriate, nor are 5" heels. Keep your jewelry small and tasteful, nothing showy that will detract attention from you.
- **For Men:** A tucked-in, button-up shirt (tie and jacket optional) is appropriate, slacks (no jeans), shoes with dark socks, no sneakers.

Interview Venue

You'll want to clarify when and how the interview will take place, in-person at an office, via remote access on computer, or via remote access by AI. Each requires a different mindset and type of preparation. Make sure ahead of time that you have the correct street address and suite or floor number (if in person) or the correct link (if remote or AI), plus contact information in case you need to reach someone on the interview day. Allow extra time for gaining entry to the building or for connecting to the remote-access site.

Remote Computer Interviews

The day before the interview, make sure you locate the e-mail that includes the Zoom or URL address for the interview stored in an easy-to-access place on your computer so you don't have to get frantic at the last minute looking for the address.

The day of the interview, make sure your computer is fully charged, that your charging cable is nearby and easily available as a backup, that you have a strong Wi-Fi signal, and that you are set up in a quiet area with no disturbances (people, animals, or outside noise).

Check the location of your computer, so that there is good light on your face without shadow. Consider the background behind you that your interviewer will be seeing and either preset your computer with a neutral background or, if you are in your local surroundings, make sure the background is neat and without distractions.

Mute all your message notifications and ringtones on all your devices (phone, tablet, and laptop). Do a sound check to make sure your microphone and your earbuds or speakers work.

If you live with others or are logging in from a shared space, make sure the others present know you will be in an important interview and cannot be disturbed (except for serious emergencies).

Prior to the interview, print out copies of your resume and the job description for easy reference.

Log on at least five minutes early to the interview. This also gives you time to make final adjustments. Never make an interviewer wait for you to log on. Better to be early than even right on time.

Once in the interview, you are on! Give everyone a warm and friendly greeting and thank them for their time.

- Good eye contact is important! (Know where your camera is and remember to look directly at it every so often).
- Smile and greet your interviewers.
- Have a notebook and pen ready to take notes.
- Write down the names of everyone in the meeting (full names if possible).
- Tell them how much you appreciate the chance to speak with them and how excited you are about the job.
- Sit up straight in your chair (no slouching). No crossed legs.
- Speak clearly and loudly enough to be heard.
- Don't let other screens or occurrences distract you from the interview.

- Keep your energy UP!
- Do not cover your face or mouth with your hands.
- Do not lean on your elbows.
- Do not fidget.

If you don't feel like you have a good response to a question, make a quick note and ask them if you can have a minute to think about your response, then give your answer.

Thank everyone at the end of the interview.

Send a thank you e-mail to your interviewers within 10 hours or less (see "Your Follow-Up Thank You" section in this chapter).

AI-Assisted Interviews

Employers are increasingly using AI to prescreen job candidates, even before they meet with a human. *Washington Post* reporter Danielle Abril[1] notes that AI can be used to evaluate candidates' communication skills, problem-solving, initiative, professionalism, and attitude. In fact, the AI system can not only conduct the on-camera remote interview but can also provide employers with feedback to help them filter out the weakest candidates.

Typically, a candidate will log on to a URL at a designated time. They will then be given a series of on-screen questions either written or video-recorded. Candidates have specified amounts of time in which to answer, generally one to several minutes.

If you know you will be having an AI interview, it's a good idea to have a clear idea of your talking points in advance and how to answer questions in a clear and complete way.

In some—but not all—cases, respondents may be allowed to rerecord their responses. While taking an AI interview can certainly be intimidating, here are some tips to help you feel more confident:

- Follow the same guidelines as mentioned previously to ensure that your technical setup is working and your lighting and background showcase you in your best light.

- What you wear matters, so keep your clothes professional, as mentioned earlier.
- Prepare your responses in advance, with an understanding of the job for which you are applying. Abril (*Washington Post*) offers the sample question, "Tell us about a time you solved a tough problem."
- Look at the camera, as you would during any interview, to showcase your best eye contact. Even though you are talking to a bot, imagine there is a real person on the other end who you are trying to connect to. Within reason, try to present a warm and at-ease side of yourself that shows you can connect with people.

Perspectives: Allyns Melendez, CEO, HR Transformed

In an online application/interview, you need to know if you are communicating with a human or a robot. If it's a human, you can be more conversational, your language can be more cordial and people oriented, and there may be a chance to ask questions.

Communicating with a bot is different. AI is looking to make connections between words. Therefore, you need to include keywords that the bot (and the hiring manager) is looking for. Include words from the job description about experience, skills, and duties that relate to your experience. Answer every question, and if the bot wants a specific format such as PDF, Word, or Excel, do exactly what it says to avoid being disqualified.

You may run into several types of video applications. One format has a Q&A that records your answers. Another asks you to present a five-minute pitch on yourself. A third format shows a question on the screen that you must answer in a minute or two, before the next question pops up. You are recorded live, so you can't go back and rerecord if you make a mistake or forget something.

Prepare by recording yourself with someone else doing a mock interview. Write down possible questions ahead and answer them.

When you play the recording back, look honestly at how you come across and how the interviewer might see you. Are you showing that you're a good match for the job? What does your body language say? What relevant aspects of yourself are you showcasing that might help you get hired? Refine your answers and timed responses. Prepare examples showing how you solved a problem or met a challenge that demonstrates relevant skills and job experience. Practice being a good storyteller. Make sure your stories are true and to the point because if you get the job, you will be put to the test.

In-Person Interviews

In-person interviews are an event! People have set aside time from their work day to meet you, and want you to present your best self.

To help you feel more confident, make sure you know the address of your interview the day before your meeting and how you will get there, including estimated travel time. Leave extra time for travel so that if something unforeseen happens, you will not be late. Allow time to show your ID and be admitted at the lobby reception desk—sometimes there's even a line to get into the building.

- Show up *early* (10 to 15 minutes).
- Try to use the bathroom before you get there, but if you need to use the facilities, ask *before* interview begins.
- Greet everyone and make eye contact. Also, read your host's body language for signs if they want to shake hands. How you shake hands is an indication of your comfort and confidence. Use a firm, but not crushing grip with the interviewer(s). A loose, wimpy handshake can work against you, so if you are not used to shaking hands, practice with friends before your interview. If your hands get sweaty from nerves, carry a tissue to dry your hands before you meet the team.
- Make eye contact throughout and smile, at least at the beginning and end.
- Bring extra copies of your resume to hand out.

- Expect several people to be in on the interview.
- Make sure you look at the person asking the question, but also look at everyone there, one after another, as you answer.

Questions You Might Be Asked

Here are some questions that you might encounter. If you are extremely nervous about interviewing, you may want to practice answering these with a partner to help you to become more comfortable, without sounding scripted.

- "Tell me about yourself (your elevator pitch)."
  - A lot of interviewers will use this as an ice breaker to allow you to share your best professional self. Applicants may mistakenly think that this means the interviewer wants to really hear about your life. *They don't!* Think about this as your "framing" statement for why you are excited about and are a great fit for this job. You should be well practiced based on your personal brand brief from Chapter 5. Other facts to consider succinctly include: what sets you apart; your outside interests that may sync with the industry you are applying for; volunteer or community service; and things that show you are multidimensional.
  - Before the interview, review the job description and then select three aspects about your experience, training, and goals that *speak to the specific job you are interviewing for.* If possible, tie them directly to items on your resume. Practice doing this and adapt your introduction for each job. For example: "My experience in retail has made me effective at connecting with customers. As an assistant account executive, this will let me help build the business." Keep your remarks under one minute.
- What interests you about *this job? (Remember, your interview is NOT about your getting any job, but the specific one for which you are interviewing.)*

- What are your areas of strengths and areas of development (weaknesses)?
- Tell me about a time when you worked through a problem or faced a difficult challenge?
- What makes you want to pursue a career in _____ (digital marketing or related field you are applying for)?
- Give an example of a time when you worked with a team. What was your role? How did you help the team succeed?
- Where do you see yourself in five years? What are your long-term career goals?
- What do you enjoy doing in your spare time?

Tips to Do Your Best

- Answer the question that was asked. Be sure to listen carefully! Frame your answer around the needs of the company, but also showcase your relevant experience.
- Have a notebook and pen handy to take notes (same as on Zoom).
- Write down the names of everyone present.
- Write down keywords to questions being asked.
- If you don't know an answer right away, ask for a moment to compose your thoughts. Then give your answer.
- Thank your interviewer(s) at the end.

Perspectives: Allyns Melendez, CEO, HR Transformed

The best questions to ask in an interview are about the job, the organization, or the interviewer, not about you. Take notes during your interview. When it's your turn to ask questions, show that you are actively listening and are picking up on what's important.

How you frame your questions matters. If you are interested in whether you would work from home or from the office, you might want to ask, "Will I need to show up to the office every week?" A better way to ask is, "What are your expectations regarding in-office work versus work from home?" In the first example, you are putting your needs over the job. The second example shows that you want to understand company expectations and deliver what they need.

Active listening is key. Listen carefully to how the interviewer is sharing information and asking questions. There are clues to each interviewer's style. If they provide a lot of details, they may want to hear more specifics from you about how you approach your experience. If they present broader ideas, it can be better to mirror their approach with bigger picture answers like, "That's interesting. Here's my thinking on how I can be an asset." Always highlight your skills and experience in ways that will resonate better with your interviewer to form a better connection.

Your Questions

Most interviewers will conduct the interview and then ask you if you have questions. You should *always* go into an interview with questions that either pertain specifically to the job or that may be more general about the company and the workplace expectations and experience.

Generally, you should be prepared with three questions. Here are a few to choose from, but you may think of others:

- What are the skills or qualities that are most important for success in this role? (Here's an opportunity to talk about what you bring that meets their needs.)
- What are your biggest challenges and priorities at this time?
- How do you measure success?
- What does a typical day look like for someone in this position?
- What is the workplace culture like?
- What drew *you* to this company?
- What do you like about working here?
- What's the reporting structure?
- How does the company balance office and work from home?

- What are the greatest challenges for entry-level professionals starting off?
- How would you describe this company in a few words?
- What are the next steps in this process, and when can I expect to hear from you?

Questions to Avoid

While some candidates want to get a sense of how competitive they are during the interview, they may inadvertently ask questions that are self-defeating. Therefore, you should *avoid* questions that call attention to your weaknesses or negatives, such as, "Do you see any weaknesses in my resume?" or "Do you think I'm competitive for this position?" These highlight your insecurities and liabilities, so avoid asking these types of questions. Focus instead on highlighting your strengths and showcasing why you are a great candidate for the job.

Likewise, you should not ask questions about work–life balance, job benefits, and salary in your first interview. This interview is not about what benefits you derive from your employer, but rather what you can bring to the job to be a productive and valued member of their team.

Ending the Interview

Thank everyone in the room even if you didn't feel the interview went well. It's often hard to read the room. *How you feel may not be how they feel!* End positively and restate your interest in the position. You can ask what are the next steps or when you might expect to hear from someone.

Your Follow-Up Thank You

While you may feel a huge sense of relief that you made it through the interview, you are still not done selling! A thank you note is another opportunity to reaffirm your interest and to highlight significant selling points that may have come up in the interview or to mention something that you may have overlooked in the interview. *Thank you notes are not optional if you want to succeed!*

Within 10 hours, send an e-mail to your main contact, and to everyone else (if you have their e-mail addresses) who was a part of your interview. Your subject line could be as simple as, "Thank You for the Interview."

Send each person a slightly different note. Keep them short and to the point. While the overall tone can be similar, try to address something unique to each person's interests. Interviewers may compare the notes they received from you. Tailoring each note to its recipient helps show that you are attuned to the different needs of the team members.

Your first line should thank them and strongly affirm your positive feelings about the interview and enthusiasm for the job. Focus on a few key points from your interview that specifically address their priorities and show how you are a strong match. If you want to address several key points, you can also bullet them to make reading easier. If you did not adequately answer a question in the interview, you can briefly add your response here.

Try to affirm something you heard your interviewers talk about that shows you understand what's important to them. If you agreed to follow up your interview with some writing samples or other documents, here is your chance to state what your next steps will be.

Proofread your notes *thoroughly* before sending. Then take some time to decompress before starting on your next application.

The Waiting Game

If you don't hear anything in a week, send the recruiter or your main contact an e-mail to affirm your continued interest and to ask when they might make a decision.

Remember, businesses have a lot going on and filling this position is unlikely to be as high a priority for them as it is for you. Besides, they often move at a slower pace in making decisions than you might like, but there are many reasons for this, so try to be patient. They may well be waiting for another manager to weigh in.

If you get another job offer while you are waiting, it is reasonable to reach out to the hiring manager to let them know that you have received another offer, but that you really want to work for them. Ask if they can give you an indication if you are still in the running for the post and if they can give you an estimate as to when they might make a decision.

Then you can go back to the other offer and ask for a short extension. This is always a delicate dance that is hard for everyone. But it's important to be proactive to get the information you need so you can make the best decision possible with the available information.

What If I Get Several Rejections?

A job rejection never feels good, and indeed it can hurt your self-esteem. But it is *not* a reason to give up. Dealing with rejection will be an ongoing part of work life and your job search. It's helpful if you can start building up a "tough skin" early on, because rejection will come sooner or later. Practice resilience. If you feel that you have a genuine relationship with a recruiter or an interviewer, you can send a follow-up note to see if they can share any feedback on your candidacy. While they may choose not to do this, it's possible that you can learn some valuable information.

You can also take some time to do your own candid reflection on your interview process. Did you perceive any weaknesses in your presentation during the interview process, or at any given time? Were you prepared for the questions? Did you ask reasonable and affirming questions? Did anyone note any weaknesses in your application?

If you do find something, this is an opportunity to learn from experience so you won't repeat the same error next time.

Keep on Keepin' on

You need to be a long-distance runner. *This is a marathon, not a sprint.* Do not give up on your network. It's your job search antenna, and there are other people who can help you. Finding a job is a matter of probabilities. The more appropriate positions you apply for, the higher the probability you'll find a good job you are excited about.

Interviewing for jobs also allows you to learn and grow, so you can go in even stronger and more confident for your next interview. If you start to feel your interviewing skills may be weak and that you keep losing out on opportunities, find someone you trust who can help you practice interviewing and who will give you candid and constructive feedback to help you improve. This can be a former professor, or someone in your network with whom you have a good relationship. *Many people feel this way at some point, but dealing with it constructively can help set you apart and let you succeed.*

Chapter Wrap Up

- Be well-prepared for an interview. It is one of the keys to your success.
- Dress professionally and show up early. For remote interviews make sure you have carefully prepared your technical set-up to ensure that things go smoothly on your end.
- Think about ways to showcase your expertise for the specific company/job that you are interviewing for, and do not talk about generic opportunities.
- Be proactive in the questions you ask to help you understand the company culture and assess if this would be a good fit for you.
- Write thoughtful and strategic thank you and follow-up letters that continue to sell you as a strong candidate.
- When you face rejection, don't let it stop you from continuing your search, and from being committed to doing better by learning from past weaknesses.

CHAPTER 8

Salary and Benefits

Only in our dreams are we free. The rest of the time we need wages.
—Terry Pratchett

Getting a job offer is a cause for joy, if not relief. Take a moment to celebrate that you got an offer and know that your career is launched! It feels really good to know that a business sees your value and wants to pay you for your skills and contributions. It is validating and affirming.

Starting Salaries

Starting salaries in marketing communications span a broad range starting at about $40,000 and reaching about $70,000.

Salary: Advertising in United States 2024 | Glassdoor[*]

Salary: Copywriter in United States 2024 | Glassdoor[†]

Salary: Marketing Digital in United States 2024 | Glassdoor[‡]

Salary: Entry Level Public Relations in United States 2024 | Glassdoor[§]

Factors that affect salary ranges include: your demonstrated competencies and experience (including internships); industry sector; location and size of the business; and external factors, such as U.S. business economic health, which can impact supply and demand for entry-level talent.

For example, jobs in some major metropolitan areas, such as New York and Los Angeles, may pay more than those in other cities. Similarly, positions at large global agencies may pay better compared

---

[*] www.glassdoor.com/Salaries/advertising-salary-SRCH_KO0,11.htm
[†] www.glassdoor.com/Salaries/copywriter-salary-SRCH_KO0,13.htm
[‡] www.glassdoor.com/Salaries/digital-marketing-salary-SRCH_KO0,17.htm
[§] www.glassdoor.com/Salaries/entry-level-public-relations-salary-SRCH_KO0,28.htm

to those at smaller boutique agencies. Specialized industries, such as financial, medical, and technology sectors may also pay higher starting salaries such as beauty and entertainment, though this is not always the case. Entry-level digital marketing salaries tend to be somewhat higher than those in other communication areas, but again, it depends on multiple overlapping factors. So do your homework.

It's Not Just About the Money

Being paid for your work is obviously an important reason to accept a job. However, the salary may not be the *most* important consideration when you are starting out. You can generally expect to get an offer between $40,000 and $55,000 depending on the company that's hiring, though some specialty areas may command a higher starting salary. In rare occasions, it may be possible to negotiate a slightly higher salary if you have interned at the organization and have a strong track record. However, for entry-level jobs, if you make negotiating for a higher salary a condition for employment, you may risk losing the job offer.

Perspectives: Ibrahim Tatlicioglu, Media Planning Supervisor, EssenceMediacom

I was lucky enough to have two job offers to choose from after graduation, one in account management and another in media strategy. Even though I didn't grasp everything that a media strategist does, there was something I just liked about that job and the people who interviewed me. Sometimes you have to go with your gut.

While the starting salary is important, money is not everything. You're going to commit a lot of time and effort to one employer, so it's more important to be excited about the job, rather than making more money to start. That will come later.

Research the Marketplace: Information Is Power

Learn what the going salary rate is before you accept the job. If the job is in New York State, or in another jurisdiction that requires job salary ranges to be disclosed, make sure you know the currently disclosed salary range for the job you were offered. This is important information that can help you to assess an offer and possibly negotiate for a better one if you are being offered a salary below what is listed.

Wage inequity continues to be an issue in today's workplace. Women earned 18 percent less than men in 2021, according to CNN.[1] To address this, several states, including New York, have laws that require businesses with five or more employees to include salary ranges for all job postings.[2] In New York, not posting the minimum and maximum salaries may result in a fine of up to $125,000 for the company.[3] As a result, you should be able to see the salary range for most New York businesses before you apply and certainly before you negotiate a possible offer.

If you are applying for work in a state that does not mandate posting salaries, you may be at an initial disadvantage in negotiating if you don't know the salary range. Start by researching similar jobs posted on Glassdoor or Fishbowl.

Without having a published salary range as a guide, if an employer asks your salary requirements, *do not offer a hard number*. This does not work to your favor, as you may state a number that is lower than the job is worth or than the company is willing to pay. You may effectively be bidding against yourself. Therefore, you would be wise, instead, to say something like, "I am looking for a competitive salary commensurate with this job's requirements and with my experience. Can you share the salary range for this job with me?"

If you have done your research to see what other comparable jobs in your field are paying, you can better assess where you fit on the scale, and how you might advocate for a higher salary than the base level.

Perspectives: Isabella Santana, Manager, Integrated Media Planning, OMD

Starting my career, I did not have a lot of power to negotiate my salary or benefits. Generally, new professionals have to accept the terms they are offered because they don't have a strong bargaining position or track record of success. However, I was very lucky: one of my references gave me a great recommendation for my first job and strongly advocated that the company pay me more. I was beyond thrilled when the employer came back with a higher offer.

When you do get a job, update your LinkedIn profile right away. After you've been on the job six to eight months, recruiters may see from your profile that you now have experience and contact you for other jobs. Many people job hop from company to company because they gain more money each time. This works for some, but make sure your skills and abilities keep pace with the higher job titles. You may find yourself out of work if you don't deliver at the expected level.

Wiggle Room: When It's Reasonable to Ask for More Money

Asking for a higher starting salary because you want it or need it for living expenses is not a strong justification for getting more money.

As an entry-level employee, you will not have much power to negotiate for a higher salary at the start. After all, the company is taking a chance on you as an untested full-time professional. Use this opportunity to get your foot in the door, get experience, learn as much as you can, and start building your professional credentials. You will more than likely use this job as a springboard to your next position, either within the company or elsewhere, where you will have more leeway to negotiate for a higher salary once you have more substantive results that showcase your value.

However, if you believe you deserve a salary on the higher end of the scale, your position will be stronger if you can provide evidence or a compelling rationale as to *why* the company should consider a higher starting salary. Beyond the stated job criteria, if you also have experience that directly reflects on your ability to perform at a higher level than expected for an entry-level post, make a list of your related experience and skills that you think merit a salary above the original offer. You lose nothing by asking the hiring manager if they would factor your additional experience into their offer.

For example, if you have a year of internship experience with that company or in a similar role, that may be justification for you to ask for more than the company's lowest offer, since you have a track record of success in the job you are going to perform.

Finding a Compromise That's Good for Both Parties

When you negotiate, you are taking a proactive stance to advocate for yourself, beyond an outright acceptance of a proposed salary offer. That means there will be one or more conversations between you and the hiring manager, and a two-way give and take.

In negotiating, both you and the company representative will work to find a reasonable compromise. As a result, it is appropriate and expected that you might even ask for 5 percent more than the minimum that you would accept. For example, if a company is offering a starting salary range of $40,000 to $52,000, and you have some substantive related experience, you might ask for $48,000, and expect a counter offer of $42,000. You may split the difference and perhaps start at $45,000. Be prepared to ask for slightly more than you might expect with the understanding that this will be a process that hopefully arrives at an equitable compromise.

If you feel that the firm salary offer is low, but you are inclined to accept the job, you can ask the hiring manager about the company policy regarding employee review, and when you might be considered for a raise. Sometimes it's possible to ask for a performance review after six months, but more than likely you'll have to wait for your annual review to see if you might be competitive for a raise. Do not expect any guarantees as to when you might get a raise. This depends on your performance and other factors that are beyond your control.

Understanding Your Benefits

While salary is the starting point, you'll also want to ask about the benefits that will accompany the salary. These will vary from company to company, but they generally include the following:

- Health and other insurance
- Vacation days/paid holidays
- Paid personal days/sick days
- Work from home (WFH) flexibility versus required days in office
- Home office equipment/supply stipends
- Phone/Internet stipend
- Retirement benefits for 401K or other plan, including possible employer matching of employee contributions to the plan
- Stipends for continued professional education and skills building
- Other life quality perks

While benefits packages are generally nonnegotiable, understanding how benefits could enhance your life could make you feel more comfortable with a lower starting salary.

You can generally expect to receive an offer letter (which may come as an e-mail, an attachment to an e-mail, an overnight delivery, or U.S. mail) that will outline your starting salary, terms of employment and benefits. Review the letter or e-mail carefully! If you have questions, now is the time to ask for clarification. Further changes may be hard to come by later.

Timing and Navigating Multiple Job Offers

It is not uncommon for competitive job seekers to face some uncomfortable timing regarding job offers for multiple positions. The good news is that you are a free agent able to change your mind. Even if you have accepted a job, signed an offer letter of employment, or made a verbal agreement, these are not legally binding.

For example, if you have accepted a job with Agency A, but prior to starting that job you get another attractive job offer from Agency B, you have options.

Option 1

If you are excited about sticking with Agency A, but Agency B offers you more money and/or better benefits, you can say "No thanks" to Agency B and let them know that you have already accepted another job offer. If you are interested, you can keep in touch for future opportunities. Be gracious. You never know when your paths may cross again.

Option 2

If you feel that Agency B's benefits/salary package is strong, you can go back to Agency A and tell them that you received another offer. Affirm to Agency A that you are committed and excited about working for them and ask if they have any flexibility to meet (or get closer to) the salary/benefits of Agency B. You can also ask if they would commit to reviewing your work in a few months to consider a salary merit increase.

Remember to always maintain your professionalism by being gracious, forthright, and courteous. You don't want to appear to be taking advantage of them or to give the impression that they are disposable.

Option 3

If you feel that Agency B's offer is so appealing that you don't want to pass it up, you have the option to accept their offer. However, this requires going back to Agency A to inform them that your circumstances have changed and you will not be moving forward working with them, even though you had an agreement.

This assumes that you have *not* started work there and have received no financial remuneration for your work with Agency A. If you have, either by salary, furnishings, equipment, moving costs, and so on, you will need to pay it back or return it in full, or risk being sued.

While this presents a potentially uncomfortable discussion, and you may feel bad about changing your mind, ultimately, you are best served by advocating for the offer that you determine is best for you at any given time.

There are no guarantees with any job, so you'll want to consider all your options, weigh advantages versus liabilities, and ultimately, you may just go with your gut.

Chapter Wrap Up

- You have researched the salary ranges of job offers and you understand a fair industry guideline for a starting job in your sector.
- You have assessed what relevant experience and skills you have and whether you have tangible justification to ask for more money.
- You understand the job benefits and how they will affect the quality of your life and work life beyond salary.

Time to get ready for Day One on the job!

CHAPTER 9

Job Success From Day One

Success is a journey, not a destination.

—Arthur Ashe

Throughout my career, I always felt that starting a new job was a major life event—a really big deal, especially early on. Because it is!

It's a huge accomplishment and affirmation to be chosen for a job from a competitive field of applicants. (Give yourself a pat on the back here.) While starting a job is exciting, it can also be scary. You might feel a little intimidated because you're starting from scratch and need to prove yourself in new ways to be successful.

If you feel that you're experiencing "imposter syndrome," fear, and self-doubt that you don't really have what it takes to do the job, STOP! That is not an unusual reaction, and you are not alone in feeling this way. Remember, just because you may doubt your abilities does not mean you can't do the job. Starting a new job means accepting that you will be learning on the job, to go above and beyond your current capabilities. An entry-level professional is hired for their potential. That means accepting you won't know everything from Day One, and that you'll learn and improve through feedback as you go.

If you start to feel self-doubt taking over, draw on your "confidence bank" to calm your nerves and help you to move forward. Here's some of what's in your bank:

- The hiring team picked *you* for the job after carefully vetting you.
- You have the foundational skills to deliver and build on.
- You have a track record of success that got you here.
- You have many personal and professional strengths (see Chapter 1).

- You have a strong network of people to support you. Phone a friend! (see Chapter 4).
- You are *not* an imposter (many people start out feeling this way), even if you don't know everything about how to do this job.

In other words, remember that you deserve to be in your position, and you can deliver! Take time to celebrate that you landed this job. Prepare yourself mentally to tackle your new role, because there's a lot of "new" coming your way: daily routine, company rules, skills to apply, stuff to learn, how to do your job effectively, people (your boss and co-workers) to get to know, an office culture and politics to figure out, and, of course, opportunities to grow.

Bring Your A-Game From Day One

Starting from Day One, you need to bring your A-game. As the saying goes, "First impressions matter." So be ready to deliver from the get-go. Here are some tips to help you start strong:

- Show up (log in) early—and keep showing up early, too.
- Connect with your boss and ask him/her/them when is a good time to meet.
- Fill out paperwork with HR and/or go through training sessions.
- Take notes (do not assume you'll remember).
- Ask questions when you don't understand something or need clarification.
- Get settled in your work station and get a sense of the workplace environment.
- Meet your team: Introduce yourself, get familiar with their names.
- Be friendly to everyone you connect with: Smile, make eye contact.
- Be especially nice to the administrative and tech support staff.
- Say please and thank you.

While you are getting acclimated, remember work life is continuing for other employees, so do not expect them to drop everything for you. This is especially true of your supervisor/boss, who will be juggling multiple tasks and may not have time to do a deep dive with you. Don't let this discourage you.

Perspectives: Allyns Melendez, CEO, HR Transformed

One of the best approaches to new job responsibilities is taking excellent notes during orientation. If you have a question, reread your briefing notes to see if the answer is there. It shows that you've done your homework before asking for help. If you have other questions, make them as specific as possible, which will help your supervisor understand what you need.

Get to know key people in your area of the company, which could include your manager, their manager, other staff, or the business owner. Create an opportunity to meet and ask general questions that show you are interested in the company's goals, not just in your own job.

Showing up ready to do your job is essential. There may be additional events beyond your job description that are opportunities to showcase your talents and engagement. There may be a brainstorming meeting that you weren't invited to, but is open to everybody. Go and participate, as long as you complete your priority work. It's important for people to see you, hear your ideas, and know that you take initiative.

Come to work as your authentic self, knowing what you bring to the table. Just about everyone at every job level has felt the "impostor syndrome" at some point. Don't copy another person's tone or style if it's not who you really are. The company hired you because of who you are. If you need to talk about your insecurities, find a mentor to work this through, especially if your supervisor is not open to talking about it or if they tend to judge rather than help. Everyone can benefit immensely from external reassurance sometimes. You can also affirm your track record to bolster your confidence, even if you are nervous about it. You won't know everything when you start any new job. The expectation is that you are always learning.

Your boss has expectations, too, including:

- You are excited to be there and are ready to get to work.
- You are new so it's okay not to know how to do everything.
- You may be going through on-boarding and training to get used to company systems.
- You will start getting acquainted with your team.
- You will ask questions.
- You will be proactive as you start to learn the ropes.
- You will have a grace period while you are getting up to full speed.
- You will quickly begin to figure things out for yourself.

There are actions you can take to maximize your entry into a new workplace. For example, during down time, get to know the internal communications and file share systems. Try to familiarize yourself with the formatting and style that your team uses to communicate with each other and with upper management. If you have down time, you can offer your help to team members.

It is a great idea to take detailed notes whenever you are given information that you need to remember. Write down your questions, too, so you can follow up later.

While questions are expected, appropriate and necessary, you also need to be respectful of other people's time. Try to get a sense of who best can help answer your questions and how much time and patience they have. At some point, you will need to start to fend for yourself.

Time Management Is Key

One of the most challenging parts of transitioning to a work place, especially in a marketing communications agency, is learning how to effectively manage your time when working on multiple client accounts.

Understanding your boss's priorities for each client is a key to helping you prioritize your tasks. That means *you need to be organized,* so you are working most efficiently. *Multitasking* is another important ability in today's workplace. You are juggling e-mail responses, client pitches, team tasks, meetings, project delays, and a myriad of other duties that you need to track and address in a timely way.

Because you are just starting out, expect that your learning curve will be steep. That means that you will spend a lot of energy, time, and effort in a short period of time (perhaps the first four months) figuring out how to do your job in a way that meets your employer's expectations. Remember, your supervisor doesn't expect you to know everything from Day One, but they *do* expect you to catch on and start delivering in a reasonable way, showing that you are learning at a steady pace and gradually taking on more responsibility.

Time management takes time and practice to learn, but the sooner you can do this, the better you'll feel, and the more successful you'll be. You will need to do this throughout your career, so invest in this now. Time management includes learning what's important, what needs to be done first and what can be done later, how long it takes to get things done, when people need things from you, how much lead time and notice people need when they have to do things for you, who needs to be consulted, and who needs to sign off. And you need to do this all while understanding that your needs may not be the top priorities of others whose input you need. It's a lot to juggle, but if you are diligent and pay attention, you can catch on pretty quickly. Just remember to breathe!

Perspectives: Susan Akinyi-Tindi, Account Director, Dieste Health

The first thing to know at a new workplace is that you don't know anything. Before you accept a job, research the company, its values, and the people who work there, especially the leadership. You may be there a long time and you need some idea of who you're working for.

As an intern at VMLY&R, my supervisors gave me grace because I was working part-time and I was a student as well. When I transitioned to full-time, it was a huge wake-up call. Expectations were different. I needed to work smarter, think about my attitude, and learn how to be resourceful and deliver for my team and client.

You need to be able to pivot, because one minute it's one thing and the next minute it's something different. You have to step up and pitch in, even if it's not your job. You have to prove that you have what it takes to be there.

One huge challenge was not always feeling certain about what I was doing. I used gut instinct and found I knew more than I thought. Managers prefer it when you come to them with solutions rather than problems. I learned to think about a solution ahead of time even if it wasn't always the best. Your boss may hold your hand for a while after your start, but then you need to start bringing something to the table.

Some days are hard and you just want to cry. Then you realize you can do it. Keep pushing and don't give up. There's always another way. Work, like life, is not always rosy, but you can celebrate your rosy moments, because there will always be good and bad days.

To Be Independent or Not?

A lot of people take pride in being "self-starters." While this is an important skill, you want to find a balance when starting a job. Starting out, there is a lot you don't know, so you need to be an active listener (see Chapter 4) to process a lot of information.

While it's normal and expected to ask reasonable questions, bugging your team or boss constantly with questions on how to do your job can be a negative. If you find yourself asking a lot of questions about something that was already explained, it may be a sign that you need to work smarter to grasp the information. Take notes and consult them when necessary. Devote some time to get comfortable with the new information. That may mean putting in additional time early on to get up to speed.

For more generic "how-to" questions, many people rely on Google searches for help. In fact, this could be one of your greatest supports. Problem-solving shows your savvy and motivation.

However, if you are advising a client or have a substantive question about content or company policy about which you are uncertain, it's always better to ask someone on your team.

Managing Up—An Essential Part of Your Tool Kit

Many people start a job thinking they just need to focus on the tasks in their job description to be successful. While working successfully on your assigned responsibilities is important, you have the power to impact your success beyond doing assigned tasks. Learning how to "Manage Up" is an important part of your success. This is a strategic tool that allows you build an effective relationship with your supervisor to help them and you be successful.

Managing Up starts with taking initiative to understand your boss's communication preferences, needs and style. Communication is key! How do they like to be approached? e-mail? Slack? DM? In person? Is there a best time of day when they prefer to hear from you? These are questions you can ask your supervisor directly. Your boss may proactively share some of their preferences, so take note. But if you are unsure, it does not hurt to ask. Also, observe the responses to different types of communication. If you notice that e-mails or voicemails go unanswered while DMs or text messages get picked up quicker, that's good information. Some people answer e-mails only early in the morning or late at night—good to know.

You never want to find yourself in a situation where you have urgent information for your supervisor but it doesn't get to them because you used a channel that they don't prioritize. You don't want to hear them say, "Why didn't you send a text (or DM or Slack)." Try to figure out their communication style ahead of time. Better yet, ask what they prefer.

Managing Up also shows that you understand how your boss prefers to be kept informed of subordinates' work flow and priorities. Do they like daily, weekly, or biweekly reports? Do they want to be briefed in meetings, via e-mail, or another channel? Do they expect you to only come to them with pressing questions, or are they more hands-on? Each person will have a different style, so try to be sensitive to their work mode and adjust accordingly.

It's helpful to know how much background and detail they like. One hands-on supervisor wants to know (and influence) every little thing while another might say, "When I ask you what time it is, don't build me a watch."

It also means being sensitive to your boss's priorities. It shows them that you are working in a way that addresses their priorities. This awareness might help you decide which client work you complete first or the project you dedicate the most time to. It might also involve offering to help your boss brainstorm if they are addressing a pressing problem.

By understanding what their priorities are, you can focus on your assigned goals in the context of supporting your supervisor's goals, a win–win situation for all. When you help your boss look good, it may help you look good as well.

Career progress within a company rarely happens without the support of your boss. Likewise, failure to manage up can create misunderstandings about your boss's expectations and can potentially put you in a less favorable light. It can also cause wasted time and effort on tasks that are not in line with your boss's or team's needs. If, for example, your boss asks you for information from another department head who does not respond to you in a timely way, you'll want to tell your boss so they can intervene.

There are times when you may have a work problem and need your boss's input before moving forward. As a rule, it's best not to present a problem to your boss as open-ended in a complaining way, and expect them to solve it. Your discussion will be stronger if you have given some thought to the issue and have some ideas about workable and suitable solutions. Your ideas may not be perfect, but by doing some thinking prior to approaching your boss with a problem, you show that you have taken initiative to think about possible solutions before going to them for help. You make yourself part of the solution instead of part of the problem.

While it can be intimidating, it's a good idea to foster two-way communication with your supervisor so that you are effectively responding to their feedback and priorities, but are also sharing your thoughts to help your team to be successful. This sometimes can mean seeking feedback about how you can do better in the future, which can be uncomfortable in the short term but can pay dividends later, since it shows you are committed to improvement.

Help! I Have a Horrible Boss!

Bosses come in all flavors, and that includes really, *really* bad ones! In fact, most professionals are not taught how to be strong, effective managers, and are left to figure it out for themselves. Some bosses are less successful than others. As a result, you may find yourself with a clunker, who (1) is a bad communicator, (2) does not give feedback, (3) will never win the Congeniality prize, or (4) does not effectively manage a team on deliverables.

First, try to determine if everyone on your team has the same problem. If so, it's likely an issue of how your boss communicates. If you are the only one with this concern, then it could be your issue. If this is the case, the best you can do is to try to understand their work style (Managing Up still applies) and look for opportunities for feedback and direction. If you work for a noncommunicator, you may want to rely on your team more heavily. If you see no way to a more effective working relationship, you ultimately may want to look for another job.

Show Up as You: That's Who Got Hired!

It's hard to be the new person on the job and to feel like you are immediately "fitting in," so you may go through an awkward stage as you figure out the lay of the land. It takes time to get used to your co-workers, your boss, and the general work vibe of the place. Be patient with yourself. But how you conduct yourself will go a long way in helping you to fit in sooner, including your being friendly to others and making eye contact.

If you are feeling insecure, take time to affirm the personal and professional qualities that make you a valued employee and good co-worker. Try to bring your authentic self to work even as you stay attuned to the workplace energy and how people interact. You want to spend some time observing and figuring out the workplace dynamics.

Workplaces have even more complex dynamics now, especially juggling WFH options with rotating in-office work days. As a result, you may be in a workplace where there is a constant flux of people who are physically around you and a variety of channels by which you communicate with your team and others.

If you are someone who feels "other" for any reason, that's okay for a time. Give yourself time to adapt. But also try to be proactive in connecting with people one-on-one, even if it's inviting them for a coffee, chatting at the office coffee bar or break room, or visiting more casually after work. Conversing about mutual nonwork activities that are popular, like what you are streaming or what podcasts or music you are listening to, is another way to build connections.

Perspectives: Andrea Weinzimer, Senior Vice President, Human Resources, Hachette Book Group

When you start a new job, there's a lot to learn about workplace expectations, asking effective questions, taking initiative as a valued and productive team member and more. The workplace is a new world that you need to learn to navigate. It will impact your growth and success beyond just doing your job.

Because of remote work, especially during Covid, new professionals may think working from home is a substitute for being in the office. They may prefer it and feel confident they can do their jobs just as well remotely. This is frequently not the case. In fact, working from home full-time can stunt your professional growth, especially as a communications professional.

While full-time in-office jobs may no longer be the norm, coming to the office at least three days a week is reasonable and benefits you as much as your employer. Virtual meetings are not a substitute for meeting face-to-face with others where you can read body language and verbal cues, see interactions, participate more proactively, and get a better understanding of what makes the company tick. Showing up also signals management that you care about the client or company beyond your own tasks. This is essential to your success.

A good workplace culture can also be fun and rewarding. Sitting next to a work colleague gives you a deeper way to form friendships beyond your job tasks. Being around other diverse professionals helps you grow, connect, and learn in important and unexpected ways. I cannot overemphasize the value of those in-person interactions.

Code Switching

Harvard Business Review defines code switching as "adjusting one's style of speech, appearance, behavior, and expression in ways that will optimize the comfort of others in exchange for fair treatment, quality service, and employment opportunities.[1]"

Putting it another way, to get ahead and feel accepted, we need to be perceived as "fitting in" to help others feel comfortable with us.

While this might apply to anyone who does not feel that their identity is reflected and affirmed in the workplace, code switching is an especially prevalent concern for people of color who may work in a primarily white workplace. While many companies are increasingly focusing on diversity, equity, inclusion, and belonging (DEIB), many are still behind the curve in fostering a truly inclusive workplace. So it's left up to the individual to determine how much they feel they can alter their demeanor to try to "fit in" to a company culture.

There are numerous studies on code switching and whether it leads to success or takes a greater personal toll on an individual. I have generally advised students, especially those of color going into a primarily white workplace, to go in with a positive attitude and to bring their best authentic professional selves, despite their trepidations.

Generally, most were successful in navigating the workplace and grew their confidence in the process, though not always.

Try to spend some time observing others to get the "vibe" of a workplace and to see how people interact. While you do not need to be and should not try to be a carbon copy of everyone else, you do want to try to make genuine connections with positive daily interactions that build relationships. Remember, your work colleagues do not need to be your friends, but you do need to find ways to be effective as a team. If they become friends, that could be a plus in your life, too.

While you may feel challenged to alter your behavior and demeanor to "fit in," if the workplace is not respectful of differences, this could also take a toll on your mental health. If there are HR or DEIB offices that are dedicated to addressing related issues, it may be worth having a conversation. And if you continue to feel disrespected, it again may ultimately be worth considering another job.

Perspectives: Susan Akinyi-Tindi, Account Director, Dieste Health

As a person of color, I felt lucky to find another person who looked like me in my job, and who could also be an ally. During the Covid pandemic, we created a peer-to-peer mentorship for people of color in the company. That helped me tap into a much broader network so I did not feel like the only person of color in the room.

I code switched a lot more when I was starting out. I used to feel like I just had to find a way to fit in. I didn't want to be the person who laughed too loud or didn't find something funny during coffee break gatherings. I can't hide my real feelings, so working at home during the pandemic worked in my favor. It's easier to be with others remotely.

But as I've gotten older and more confident in my skills and my position, I no longer see the need to code switch, because I feel that people need to take me as I am. My work speaks for itself.

I do know senior professionals who still code switch, but the thing to remember is that at some point in your career this will shift for you. I still find it difficult to always be the only person of color in the room or on my team. That's why I actively encourage more people of color to join the industry through outreach programs.

Clients are increasingly demanding more people of color on their teams. I was confident I could bring value because my clients knew I understood their audience by living and breathing who they are.

Good Enough Is Not Good Enough

Most jobs offer criteria by which you will be measured for your annual reviews. Some will even give you clear metrics to evaluate your performance. While it's important to be aware of how your success will be measured and to think about ways to showcase the value of your work, I've learned that *to really succeed, being good enough is not good enough*. That means that if you want to stand out, get promoted and make your mark in the workplace, you can't just check the boxes and deliver the basics. It's a given that you will do your job. But to get ahead means going above and beyond to deliver tangible value to your team and others with whom you work.

You can do this by proactively contributing strategic ideas to team brainstorming, keeping your team abreast of important trends and breaking news that may impact current work, offering to do additional work on an initiative to support your boss and team projects, and working on projects that support your supervisor's success, too (see Managing Up).

When you think about your own workplace success, try to look at your work from your boss's perspective and priorities to determine if you are doing more than checking boxes for your own tasks. Harder to do, but it will help you to stand out and show you bring value beyond your defined role.

Do Your Own Internal PR (Even If You Are Not a PR Professional)

Many young pros just starting out in the workplace assume that if they just work hard and do their job, their supervisors will be aware of their contributions and efforts and will see them in a favorable light, especially around annual review time.

Don't assume that this will happen.

Supervisors are busy and are focused on their own responsibilities, even if they are responsible for your work assignments. As a result, it's up to you to keep an ongoing record of your successes, tangible contributions, and encounters that affirm your value and, if possible, show that you are going above and beyond to deliver. Remember, trying hard is not what matters. Results are.

This is especially true for your annual review.

Here are a few tips to help showcase the great work you do on a regular basis:

Keep your own file of your positive encounters with others in the company and clients or other important stakeholders. This is one way to gather evidence of your value, especially for your annual review.

Do not assume that you will remember all the successes you have along the way over the course of a year. If you have a designated file system on your successes, you can gather the responses as evidence of your value to include with the evidence of the hard deliverables that your boss expects from you.

Share significant ongoing positive feedback you get from other stakeholders with your boss via e-mail. If you score a major coup with a client or receive outstanding feedback, send your supervisor a "good news" e-mail saying something like, "I'm happy to report that our client was especially enthusiastic with the report on X and will be moving forward with my recommendations. This was a key objective for our team and I'm glad I could contribute to our efforts."

When the Crap Hits the Fan: Keep a CYA Memo File

Sometimes office politics get nasty and there can be finger pointing and blame if things don't go as planned. If this is the case, it's a good idea for you to write a note *to yourself,* sometimes called a CYA (*Cover Your Ass*) memo, that recounts the facts as you remember them. Do not lie about the facts. To the best of your ability, document times, dates, participants of meetings, and critical decision points, so that you can clearly present your role in the matter, which could help prevent or lessen negative fallout for you. Save it in a private place so that it's for your reference only (ideally not on the shared company computer network), but can be pulled out if you are drawn into a messy situation and need to be able to clearly explain your role. Better to document an occurrence when fresh than to trust your memory.

What If I Screw Up?

People are fallible and we all make mistakes. It's important to try to avoid small careless errors in your everyday work by paying close attention to detail and by carefully reviewing, fact checking, and proofreading your work before sharing it with others. While a small error here or there may not be grounds for being fired, a significant number of careless errors *can be* grounds for getting fired. Train yourself to build in extra time to ensure that all your work is as perfect as you can deliver it. And if you find that your supervisor is consistently noting errors, address the issue now and figure out what you need to do differently.

If you are responsible for a major error that is highly visible and has potential to negatively impact your team, supervisor, or client, you'll want to acknowledge your role, even if you feel really bad.

If this is an error you discover, tell your supervisor as soon as you realize it and, if need be, ask for guidance to address it. If it's an error that you made, but can correct on your own, you may also want to share it with your supervisor so they hear about it from you and not from someone else.

If your boss wants to meet with you to discuss the problem, the best thing to do is to acknowledge your responsibility. Make sure you don't just use the meeting to explain your actions. Listen carefully to your boss so they can share their concerns and guide you on how to not let this happen again, and you will be better able to assess how serious the damage is and how it might impact your job. Even if you are uncomfortable or feel embarrassed, try not to come across as defensive. Listen attentively to the feedback and address it as best as you can.

You need to understand how the problem happened and what you can do to ensure that this does not happen again. Showing that you take responsibility, understand the possible fallout, and have learned what to do to prevent future gaffes can possibly mitigate your being fired, especially if it's a first offense.

Office Politics: They're Everywhere

Office politics are a factor in every office. They center on who has the power to make decisions, who has influence, and where alliances lean. The better you understand that they exist and, even more, who has the power or the influence, the better you will be able to navigate the workplace.

While new and lower level employees are not generally "players" in office politics, it's good to be aware of who has the power. This can guide you in how to engage with this person or people, and in knowing whom not to cross. As a general guideline, it's best *not* to insert yourself into the drama. As a new employee, focus on just doing your job well.

I learned office politics the hard way on my first day doing PR for NBC News. I casually introduced myself to a person who worked a few doors down from me. I told them my name and who I reported to. Their immediate response was, "You just made your first mistake." I was totally baffled and dumbstruck. They invited me into their office, closed the door, and proceeded to explain to me that I should never ally myself with anyone, even my boss, because you don't know where people's allegiances lie. It turned out that this person was not a fan of my boss. While I did not do anything overtly wrong, I learned the hard way to be hyper aware of what I said and whom I said it to.

Office gossip is a mainstay of many office cultures, and while everyone enjoys hearing juicy news, it's a good idea *not* to spread gossip. That includes bad-mouthing other co-workers and supervisors in the office, even in the office rest room! You never know who is listening. Be especially careful about writing negative things in Slack or other DM channels. There are many horror stories about people inadvertently sending their negative message to the person they were bad-mouthing! Better not to say it, or not to put anything negative in writing. As the saying goes, "Loose lips sink ships." Don't be one of the negative rumor spreaders, and try to keep a reasonably neutral stance when connecting with co-workers. Never put anything negative about anyone in an e-mail or in writing.

Be a Reformer, Not a Revolutionary

One of the most important lessons I learned is that employees are hired to deliver for companies. Companies do not exist to make employees' lives better. While your pay check, happiness, and job satisfaction (not necessarily in that order) are essential to your well-being, your ability to deliver great work to help your employer meet their objectives is what matters to them, even as many employers seek to create welcoming workplaces that value employees.

That means that HR offices exist for the benefit of the company, even if there are protocols for employees to register complaints. If you don't agree with a policy or situation at your job, while you may feel that there are injustices, you will be more effective if you try to raise the issue in a measured and professional way rather than demanding change, even if you feel strongly that you are in the right.

You can do this by working your way up the ladder, starting with your boss (unless they are the problem), or potentially going to HR or your DEIB office with a document that explains the issue of concern and includes clear evidence of a transgression. If there is an issue that you feel is pervasive, you will get further trying to offer up solutions, rather than demanding change.

Change generally comes slowly to most companies, so you'll have to be patient. But if you like your job and the company you work for, it's not unreasonable to approach senior management with a legitimate issue that could affect your ability to do your job better and, even more, that could make the workplace better for others besides yourself. Just remember to pick your battles.

Perspectives: Tasha Gilroy, Global Chief Belonging Officer, VML

As much as agencies strive to create equitable, inclusive, and diverse workplaces that support employees, some managers may not be effective in connecting with you as a person, or may have difficulty connecting in some situations. They may slip and say things that are not right, or unfortunately, may make decisions about you and your work based on bias. Those situations are hard, especially at the start of your career. You may not feel equipped for a difficult conversation with your manager because you want to build a positive relationship. Even sharing constructive feedback with a boss can be challenging.

If you encounter a situation of bias or microaggression, the most important step you can take is telling someone. Do not keep it to yourself. Reach out to a colleague, manager, mentor, or leader, inside or outside your company, whom you trust to talk through the situation confidentially, at least at first. If you go to HR, ask for advice on how to address the situation with the manager. The key is not to let your feelings fester because, over time, they can build to a breaking point and can hurt your job performance. If you have tried to address the situation, but it's not getting better, you will have to make some hard decisions about your career options.

Your Work/Life Balance Matters

Increasingly, because of social media, and especially the nature of digital media, where a 24/7 world is the norm, you will want to take care that there is a clear separation between your work day and your nonwork life.

This can especially become a concern if your supervisor, co-workers, or clients do not respect boundaries regarding the end of your work day. A number of agencies, in an effort to serve clients, impose on employees well after their work day has ended, or on weekends, on an ongoing basis, requiring them to "be on" and available to work and respond to e-mails, DMs, or phone calls.

While it may be reasonable in a crisis situation to have to pitch in and do extra work beyond designated hours, this practice is not sustainable on an ongoing basis. If you find that you are in a work culture that disrespects your work boundaries, it may be worth having a conversation with your supervisor to discuss your concerns. If you can go into the conversation with a solution, even better.

When to Move On

Early in your career, you may find yourself changing jobs relatively frequently, perhaps every two years, or even more often. The key guideline to keep in mind when you're starting your career is: *If you have stopped learning and have mastered your job tasks, it's probably time to move on to another job, either within the company or with a different employer.*

Generally, you want to stay at company at least one or two years with increasing responsibilities. That could mean a promotion to a job with broader responsibilities at the company where you work, or it could mean a promotion by going to another company. If you find yourself complacent and coasting, and if the job market offers other opportunities, it could be worth putting out feelers to see what might be next even before two years. Change, while hard, is better than complacency.

Perspectives: Genesis Flores, Production Coordinator, Music Industry

I've had to do a lot of advocating for myself in my jobs. That takes believing in yourself. You often won't get the affirmation you want. When I deliver excellent work, whether my boss acknowledges it or not, I take a moment and physically pat myself on the back. It helps me to keep going.

You also need to know when to leave a job, even if it's hard. At one job, I felt that I was not being paid enough, and was turned down for a promotion despite doing the job more senior to mine. Since I liked my job and my team, I gave them several opportunities to make good, even though it was disappointing to be turned down. I kept my LinkedIn profile up to date, so when a recruiter offered me a higher paying job with more responsibility, I realized that while I had learned a lot, I needed to keep growing. Although it was a tough choice, I moved forward with a new opportunity.

Chapter Wrap Up

- Your workplace success depends on many factors and does not happen overnight, but there is a lot in your power to help you be successful.
- You are adapting to the workplace, building strong channels of communication with your boss and your team, and you understand the bigger workplace environment to help you to be successful.
- You go into a job knowing that your authentic self and your professionalism are two of the most important factors that will shape your success in the workplace. But they are not guarantees that the job will be a great fit for you.
- You are taking ownership of the job you do, and are prepared to be your own best advocate.

CHAPTER 10

Reality Check: How Business Expectations Differ From the Classroom

Toto, I've a feeling we're not in Kansas anymore.

—Dorothy in "The Wizard of Oz"

Stepping into the marketing communications workplace for the first time and learning how to navigate that world has a lot in common with Dorothy in *The Wizard of Oz*. Hopefully, it did not take a cyclone to drop you into your first job, as Dorothy was transported to Oz. After all your studying and preparation, you landed the job on *your* power.

Nevertheless, nothing can totally prepare you for what it feels like to enter a demanding workplace and navigate the Yellow Brick Road to career success. Every workplace culture, team, and job presents different rewards and challenges, and no one size fits all. You may encounter some of what Dorothy ran into along the way. Here's a preview of what you might expect, so put on your ruby slippers.

With luck, you'll work with a great team of professionals who welcome you, as Dorothy was warmly welcomed by the Munchkins. You'll want to find strong advocates, like Dorothy did in Glinda (the Good Witch of the East) and find friends and allies, as Dorothy found in the Scarecrow, the Tin Woodsman, and the Cowardly Lion. They can even help you deal with your "imposter syndrome" feelings. They, too, started out insecure about their abilities, until they discovered that they actually had what it took to succeed all along, just as you will.

Like Dorothy, you'll find some unexpected and wonderful adventures along the way (talking trees!), perhaps by working with some inspiring professionals and clients, or by feeling satisfaction from a job well done and taking pride in your own growth and professional development.

And like Dorothy, you may encounter some big challenges. Not everyone you work with will be a champion and supporter. You may have days where you feel intimidated or even menaced by clients, bosses, or co-workers, like Dorothy was by the flying monkeys or the Wicked Witch of the West. As Dorothy and her friends learned, you'll need your head, heart, and courage to find effective ways to confront those challenges.

You may even encounter your own Wizard of Oz, who appears to be a powerful force for good, but doesn't deliver on the promises made, perhaps by reneging on a promised promotion or raise.

Most importantly, like Dorothy, you have the power to reach your goals, thanks to your own ruby slippers, found in your professional brand and in the person you are. That is your secret power, which will be with you throughout your career.

Perspectives: Allyns Melendez, CEO, HR Transformed

One big difference between work and college is that at school, you can reset every semester: new classes, new learnings, new professors, and new schedule. Meeting with interns or new hires, I often hear, "I miss school." What they miss is the newness. Once you get the hang of a job, it does not have the same refresh level. You're not jumping to a new department every four months. That's a major shift in expectations and in daily life. Suddenly you're doing the same thing every day, until you get promoted or move on. That's a huge change!

There are a few things that can help you through the transition. Create some variety in your personal life. Embrace newness through activities that you love, such as reading, sports, or hobbies. If you miss the dynamic life of college, create that in your personal life. You can also bring variety to your workplace life by joining employee groups, such as social action, book clubs, culture committees, or others, so you meet new people and experience other aspects of the workplace.

Another big difference is that your supervisor is not your professor. You're expected to deliver excellent work without a lot of room for failure. You'll be judged on your performance and initiative, so there's more pressure. Unlike school, you don't get credit for trying hard, redoing assignments or handing in work late. In the workplace, if you don't deliver, you may only get a few shots to make the grade.

A New Mindset

One of the biggest wake-up calls that recent graduates encounter when they enter the workplace is transitioning from being a client, as a tuition-paying student, to working for an employer who pays you to deliver excellent work according to expectations. As a student, *you* are the client who pays the college in return for a quality education to prepare you for a communications career. You're paying to receive knowledge, guidance, and opportunities. You have the leeway to make mistakes, to hand in work late, skip a class or an assignment, redo papers, and maybe even negotiate with your professor for a better grade.

This changes when you enter the workplace. While there is some leeway to make errors when you start a job, you are expected to catch on quickly and to deliver excellent work. Excuses will not take you far. While a passing C grade may be acceptable in college, doing mediocre work will not help you be successful in the workplace. The expectation is that you will deliver A grade work all the time.

Perspectives: Ibrahim Tatlicioglu, Media Planning Supervisor, EssenceMediacom

The most important thing you can do in the workplace is to be in charge of your own narrative, how you carry yourself, and how you express yourself. That includes managing up to deliver for your supervisor and even stepping up to do tasks that may be outside your job description, but that you need to figure out how to deliver.

Keep a positive attitude and avoid being a complainer, even when you're right. How you present yourself will ultimately matter most in controlling your narrative. Interactions between people may be the most important thing and the hardest to manage, especially when you work from home. I recommend going into the office several days a week to be around others and to let them get to know you.

Good Intentions Are Not Enough

As a student, professors will often give you extra points when they see you are genuinely trying. In the workplace, however, effort and good intentions don't matter if you are not delivering.

Early on, I learned that being a dedicated employee is not enough to be successful and that you have to evolve in other ways, too. In my first job as a publicist for an artist management agency, I have a vivid memory of my boss, Mr. Barrett, angrily leaving my office, yelling. "You're too nice!" I was crushed and confused. In my naiveté, I thought that being "nice" was an important and positive quality. In retrospect, I realized that *just* "being nice" was not enough to be an effective employee. He wanted me to "toughen up" and be a more forceful advocate for our clients and our business.

While getting criticized was painful, I realized I needed to be less passive. That's hard to do, especially early on when you might feel insecure. But like any muscle that is weak, it takes focused effort to strengthen it. I had to consciously practice being more assertive and find a way to be more forceful to get results. No one could teach me how to do it. I had to figure it out by trying. It took years of practice.

Perspectives: Esraa Elzin, Influencer + Social Lead, Brand Marketing, Instacart

No matter how confident you are, getting constructive feedback from your supervisor is one of the best ways to become a better professional and deliver better work. At first, fear of criticism is normal. No one enjoys hearing they did a bad job. It stings and feels personal. I learned that when my work is criticized, it is not about me personally, it's about helping me do my job better. I have learned to compartmentalize criticism and not let it affect my sense of self or who I am outside of work. My skin is definitely thicker from learning to accept criticism.

I now seek out feedback from my boss. I don't wait for a semiannual or annual review. I ask for feedback regularly because it's in everyone's interest for me to do my job better. Giving my boss constructive feedback is also important. It's harder when you're starting out, but bosses often appreciate it too.

Learning to Juggle What's Beyond Your Control

In school, there is a lot within your control regarding managing your time and choosing courses to manage your workload. However, once you enter the workforce, you lose most of that control. In most marketing communications jobs, you'll wear many hats. That could mean having multiple job responsibilities, reporting to several people with competing priorities, serving multiple clients, or working on several projects with competing deadlines, on top of getting used to working with a variety of personalities and work styles. Learning how to set priorities, manage deadlines, adapt to multiple work styles, and be flexible to address last-minute changes is essential.

Having open communication with your boss can help to define priorities. Paying close attention is also important to gain insight into priorities, by observing what you hear and see around you. For example, if your boss consistently asks about your progress on a particular project, that's a good indication that it's important to them, even if not explicitly stated. Or if you see everyone on your team scrambling for a particular client, that's a sign of where your energies might be needed. Asking trusted team colleagues for guidance can be another way to identify top priorities. Co-workers with more experience can provide insights into how they manage priorities as a roadmap for you. And, if you are really in the dark, don't assume you can just figure it out. Ask for guidance.

Perspectives: Domonique Chaplin, MS, Public and Media Relations Manager, NYU Langone Health

As a student you have the luxury to try, fail, and learn over time, to procrastinate on homework and talk your way into an extension. The workplace is less forgiving.

Whether you are an intern, entry-level associate, or manager—you are expected to bring your professional self, ready to deliver assignments on time and to offer solutions to problems. Late or poorly executed work can cost a company business and, potentially, your job.

Starting out, time management and juggling multiple projects can be challenging. Your team understands that you are new and they don't expect you to know everything from Day One. What they do expect is that you'll ask for help when you need it. This was a humbling realization for me.

It took meeting my first big deadline by the skin of my teeth to realize that what distinguishes a professional from a student is not years of experience, but rather the ability to ask for help in a constructive way. Doing your job well doesn't just involve you anymore; it involves a larger team.

In the workplace, the quality of your work affects your employer's success. As a result, your "good grades" are based on not only the value you personally bring but also how well you support your colleagues.

With so much "new" to deal with, it's easy to feel overwhelmed when you first start out. Accept that you will need time to acclimate to a steep learning curve in the beginning, as you learn the ropes. Finding an effective project management program to help you to prioritize and track deadlines is important, along with connecting with senior staff to get tips on how they manage and streamline their workflow.

One of the most important investments you can make is through the formal and informal workplace alliances you create. Think of this as your internal support network. These are individuals to whom you do not directly report or even necessarily work with, but with whom you have a positive working relationship.

This is where your *other* PR skills come into play. Building positive working relationships helps you open communications with others who might have important information or perspectives that could help you succeed. Formal relationships may include professionals who work in HR, IT, or on another team. Informal relationships are those connections you make with other people beyond their designated role because you have a personal relationship. Both can be important allies in getting information that might not be obvious. Do not underestimate the value of having work allies to help you navigate the workplace.

When people are helpful or even just friendly, be sure to reciprocate. If you help them out when you can, you'll be more likely to have a positive "balance" in the "favor bank" when you need it and they'll be more likely to help you out in the future.

Perspectives: Susan Akinyi-Tindi, Account Director, Dieste Health

Network, network, network the hell out of your job, before you try to advance. Make sure everyone knows you in some capacity, because those are the people who will be speaking highly of you when you're not there.

The first thing I did at my agency internship was to meet other agency professionals outside my group who gave company seminars. I sent quick follow-ups thanking them for the talk and asking if I could pick their brains to go deeper into what they were talking about. People started remembering my name.

I can't count the number of times that I was added to a client pitch team just because someone knew I took great notes or had insightful things to say. People will often say things just to be heard, without adding substance. Don't speak just to speak unless you can add value.

Unlike school, where you are given a syllabus for every course with clear deadlines and deliverables, you will likely be working in a constantly shifting environment that requires you to quickly pivot and adapt to changing priorities that are beyond your control. Your formal and informal networks may be able to help.

Perspectives: Melanie Rakita, Vice President and Chief Human Resource Manager L3Harris Technologies

Education is one step in building the credibility to be successful in corporate America, but in my professional experience, what makes students successful in college bears little resemblance to what makes them successful in the working world.

I believe the keys to success in the corporate world are the same no matter where you work. Industry prioritizes resilience and learning agility. It's less about having specific experience and more about a demonstrated ability to learn, be resourceful, and recover.

College forces you to interact with people from different backgrounds but it's important to seek out environments that help you see the world through a different lens.

Be selective when joining an organization. If you're passionate about what you do, believe in what the company does and stands for and the company's culture matches your values, you're much more likely to be successful.

Join a company where you can be your authentic self. It's natural to want to make a good impression but that doesn't mean you lose sight of who you are or come at the expense of your personality. You'll be happier if you embrace who you are versus trying to project an image you think someone wants ... and more importantly you'll end up working in an environment where you fit in.

School is predictable, work is not. Ability to adapt to change is a huge predictor of success.

In the office, there's rarely an answer key. Expect everything to be grayer, and know that no matter how much you plan, something will come up that you didn't predict and be prepared to deal with it. Do what you say you're going to do. Be dependable. Take initiative. Volunteer for assignments beyond your defined scope of work. Seek out projects and perspectives, even when they may seem challenging or less than desirable.

Don't expend energy trying to convince people that you're good —show them instead.

Don't underestimate the power of relationships. Start building your network now—at all levels of your organization. Relationships are how you're going to get work done and how you'll build a future team of your own. Over time, success becomes less about what you do and more about your ability to build, develop, and deploy a team.

Knowing how to ask questions of your supervisor in a clear and concise way that will let them understand how they can help is essential. That means succinctly explaining the challenge you are facing and how they can help you solve that problem, especially if you are uncertain about how to proceed with an assigned task.

Additionally, it is key to proactively keep your supervisor informed if you have problems meeting a deadline, understanding priorities or delivering on an assignment.

Putting It All Together

While college courses and internships provide you with skills and knowledge to enter the workplace, nothing can totally prepare you for being an employee. Once you are a full-time employee, your cumulative skills and experience, coupled with your savvy, your ability to work with others, and your resilience despite setbacks, all come into play.

Being your own best advocate is perhaps one of the most important qualities you can bring to a job beyond delivering quality work. That means taking responsibility as the professional you aspire to be, delivering excellent work that supports your team's efforts and taking initiative to bring substantive ideas to help your client and employer.

This book is by no means a comprehensive guide that guarantees your success in the workplace. But it is my hope that it does contain wisdom, helpful tips, and sound advice that can help you move forward with greater confidence in your career. While these pages offer general guidance, sometimes you'll just have to experience a workplace situation to understand the complexities and how to respond—learning by doing.

Your personal brand values that you identified at the start of this book, course learnings, internships, and prior workplace experience are the core elements that you will draw on to build your success.

There is no single recipe that can guarantee your success in any job or career. You will be fueled by the person you are, the skills you acquire, the opportunities and risks you choose to pursue, the people you bring into your network, and especially by your confidence and your resilience to keep achieving your potential and dreams.

Don't ever sell yourself short. I wish you every success.

Appendix

Resources for Student Professional Development and Internships

Advertising Club of New York (ACNY) Foundation
[www.theadvertisingclub.org/foundation]

AdColor Futures [adcolor.org/futures]

AdFellows [adfellows.com]

American Advertising Federation (AAF) [www.aaf.org/Public/Public/Education
-and-Resources/Student/Student_Resources.aspx?hkey=d6029e10-a6a3
-49ca-bedf-630b3c3f9b64]

ANA Education Foundation (AEF) [aef.com/building-talent/made/made
-internship-program/made-students]

Black Public Relations Society of America (BPRS) [careers.nbprs.org/jobseekers/
internships]

BPRS NY [bprsnewyork.com/home]

BPRS Chicago [chicagobprs.com]

BPRS Detroit [nbprsdetroit.org]

BPRS LA [bprsla.org]

Center for Communications [www.centerforcommunication.org]

ColorComm [www.colorcommnetwork.com]

COOP Careers [coopcareers.org]

Emma Bowen Foundation [www.emmabowenfoundation.org]

Hispanic Public Relations Association (HPRA) [hprausa.org/hpra-scholarships]

International Radio and Television Society (IRTS) [irtsfoundation.org/academic
-programs/irts-summer-fellowship-program]

LAGRANT Foundation [www.lagrantfoundation.org]

Marcus Graham Project [marcusgrahamproject.org]

Multicultural Advertising Internship Program (MAIP) (sponsored by the American
Association of Advertising Agencies 4A's) [www.maipmatters.aaaa.org]

New York Women in Communications [nywici.org/advance/students/scholarships]

One Club [www.oneclub.org/education]

Public Relations Student Society of America (PRSSA) [www.prsa.org/prssa]

T. Howard Foundation [www.t-howard.org/students]

Where are All the Black People [www.waatbp.org]

Partial List of Industry Sites That List Marketing Communication Agencies

PR News & PR Firm Rankings [www.odwyerpr.com]

Top Advertising Agencies in the USA [www.goodfirms.co/advertising-companies/usa]

Top 30 Digital Advertising Agencies [www.webdesignrankings.com/top-30-digital-advertising-agencies]

Ultimate List of Agency Holding Companies & Their Affiliates [www.winmo.com/agency-new-business/the-ultimate-list-of-agency-holding-companies-their-affiliates]

Notes

Chapter 2

1. Sandberg and Scovell (2013), p. 53.
2. "Public Relations Firms Database—Specialty Index." (n.d.) O'Dwyer's PR News.

Chapter 3

1. "Fact Sheet #71: Internship Programs Under the Fair Labor Standards Act." (n.d.) U.S. Department of Labor.

Chapter 4

1. Williams and Cooney (1994).
2. Thaler and Koval (2006).

Chapter 5

1. Alabi (2023).

Chapter 7

1. Abril (2023).

Chapter 8

1. Goodwin (2021).
2. Haag (2022).
3. Iyer (2022).

Chapter 9

1. McCluney et al. (2019).

References

Abril, D. "Your Next Job Interview Could Be Judged by AI. Here's How to Prepare." March 27, 2023. Washington Post. washingtonpost.com/technology/2023/03/27/ai-assessed-job-interview

Alabi, T. "Why Networking is Important [+ How to Get it Right]." 2023. Hubspot.com. blog.hubspot.com/sales/why-networking-is-important

"Fact Sheet #71: Internship Programs Under the Fair Labor Standards Act." n.d. U.S. Department of Labor. https://www.dol.gov/agencies/whd/fact-sheets/71-flsa-internships

Goodwin, J. March 24, 2021. "It's Equal Pay Day: Women Lose an Average of $406,000 to the Wage Gap in Their Lifetime." CNN. cnn.com/2021/03/24/success/equal-pay-day-women

Haag, M. October 28, 2022. "What's the Salary? N.Y.C. Job Seekers Can No Longer Be Kept in the Dark." The New York Times. nytimes.com/2022/10/28/nyregion/nyc-salary-transparency-job-postings.html

Iyer, K. January 15, 2022. "New York City to Require Employers to Post Salary Ranges in Job Postings to Help Close the Pay Gap." CNN. cnn.com/2022/01/15/us/nyc-law-mandatory-salary-ranges/index.html

McCluney, C.L., K. Robotham, S. Lee, R. Smith, and M. Durkee. November 15, 2019. "The Costs of Code-Switching." *Harvard Business Review*. https://hbr.org/2019/11/the-costs-of-codeswitching

"Public Relations Firms Database—Specialty Index." n.d. O'Dwyer's PR News. odwyerpr.com/pr_firms_database/index_specialty.htm

Sandberg, S. and N. Scovell. 2013. *Lean In: Women, Work and The Will to Lead,* A.A. Knopf.

Thaler, L.K. and R. Koval. 2006. *The Power of Nice: How to Conquer the Business World With Kindness.* Crown Currency.

Williams, T. and J. Cooney. 1994. *The Personal Touch; What You Really Need to Succeed in Today's Business World.* Warner Books, Inc.

About the Author

Lynn Appelbaum is a PR professional and professor whose career spans 40 years across multiple industries and organizations. As Professor Emerita, The City College of New York (CCNY), Lynn is a nationally recognized educator and advocate for diversity in the media professions. She was named *Educator of the Year* by the Public Relations Society of America (PRSA). For her contributions to promote inclusivity in the PR profession, she was honored by the Hispanic Public Relations Association with the *BRAVO Educator of the Year* award.

Through her research on multicultural PR practitioners in the workplace and advocacy for her students, she is a long-time proponent of fostering diversity within the media professions. She continues to mentor students and young professionals independently and through the COOP Careers program.

Lynn is a Fellow and Accredited Public Relations (APR) professional of PRSA and has served on the New York Chapter and National boards of directors. She is the founding faculty member and was long-time adviser for CCNY's Chapter of the Public Relations Student Society of America.

As a practitioner for 14 years, Lynn was Press Manager for NBC News *Today* show, Director of Public Affairs for The Cooper Union for the Advancement of Science and Art, Marketing Director for Merkin Concert Hall, and Press Manager for NYU's Tisch School of the Arts and School of Law, all based in New York City.

She holds a BM from Ithaca College and MA in Arts Administration from Indiana University. She lives in New Jersey with her husband Joe Spivack and has two daughters.

Index

OTHER TITLES IN THE BUSINESS CAREER DEVELOPMENT COLLECTION

Vilma Barr, Consultant, Editor

- *Working in Business and Finance* by Joseph Malgesini
- *Make Your Internship Count* by Marti Fischer
- *Sales Excellence* by Eden White
- *How to Think Strategically* by Greg Githens
- *Succeeding as a Young Entrepreneur* by Harvey Morton
- *The Intentional Mindset* by Jane Frankel
- *Still Room for Humans* by Stan Schatt
- *Am I Doing This Right?* by Tony D. Thelen, Matthew C. Mitchell and Jeffrey A. Kappen
- *Telling Your Story, Building Your Brand* by Henry Wong
- *Social Media Is About People* by Cassandra Bailey and Dana M. Schmidt
- *Pay Attention!* by Cassandra M. Bailey and Dana M. Schmidt
- *Remaining Relevant* by Karen Lawson
- *The Road to Champagne* by Alejandro Colindres Frañó
- *Burn Ladders. Build Bridges* by Alan M. Patterson

Concise and Applied Business Books

The Collection listed above is one of 30 business subject collections that Business Expert Press has grown to make BEP a premiere publisher of print and digital books. Our concise and applied books are for...

- Professionals and Practitioners
- Faculty who adopt our books for courses
- Librarians who know that BEP's Digital Libraries are a unique way to offer students ebooks to download, not restricted with any digital rights management
- Executive Training Course Leaders
- Business Seminar Organizers

Business Expert Press books are for anyone who needs to dig deeper on business ideas, goals, and solutions to everyday problems. Whether one print book, one ebook, or buying a digital library of 110 ebooks, we remain the affordable and smart way to be business smart. For more information, please visit www.businessexpertpress.com, or contact sales@businessexpertpress.com.